CHURCH STREET

CHURCH STREET

THE SUGAR HILL OF JACKSON, MISSISSIPPI

Grace Sweet & Benjamin Bradley

THE History PRESS

Published by The History Press
Charleston, SC 29403
www.historypress.net

All photos courtesy of the authors unless otherwise noted.

First published 2013
Second printing 2014

Manufactured in the United States

ISBN 978.1.62619.111.2

Library of Congress CIP data applied for.

Contents

Acknowledgements

In borrowing from an old African proverb, "It takes a whole village to raise a child." It took interviews from people from all walks of life to authenticate and compile this research about those glorious days of Church Street. This research would not have been possible without the knowledge and assistance of many people. Amazingly, the central theme of the interviews was basically the same—namely, that Church Street was a street of extraordinary people that prevailed in a climate of Jim Crowism and unequal opportunities. Even state laws were designed to take away the dignity of these people. Yet during this period, African Americans on Church Street progressed both economically and educationally above the norm.

A special thanks is extended to the Mississippi History and Archives Commission for maintaining microfilms of the *Jackson Advocate* and the *Mississippi Enterprise* newspapers. Editor/publisher Percy Greene of the *Jackson Advocate*, in his news column "Up and Down Farish Street," informed readers on a weekly basis about the activities of the professional African Americans. He wrote about the teachers, soldiers, lawyers, doctors, preachers and nightclub owners. He also informed readers about African American life in urban cities, namely Chicago.

Editor Sarah Harvey Stevens informed readers about the social life of the African Americans in Jackson, Mississippi. She wrote about fashions, homes, church activities and social clubs and the activities of the common people of Jackson. Stevens also catered to the very young—she was Santa Claus on Christmas and Peter Rabbit on Easter. She played these roles for many years. In later years, Stevens, of the *Mississippi Enterprise*, also became the Negro editor for the "Negro News" in the *Jackson Daily News*. Many times, the same news stories about African Americans appeared in both papers. Willie Miller was the publisher of the *Mississippi Enterprise*.

Our research relied heavily on the writings of editors Percy Greene and Sarah Harvey Stevens. We extend special appreciation to those editors and their surviving family members.

We extend a special appreciation to the family of the late legendary photographer Richard H. Beadle. Specifically, we thank Dr. Jeanne Middleton Hairston and her lovely aunt, Mrs. Barbara Beadle Barber, for their unselfishness in allowing us to use the picture of the Penguin Café and the picture of Walter Duke Williams and his Concerned Committee.

We thank the family of Gertrude Hatch, whose daughters through marriage gave rise to the Conic and Speech families. We especially thank Willie Speech and his brother David Speech for the Conic family's pictures and other valuable documentation. It was through the eyes of these two brothers that we were able to realize the many contributions and achievements of the Conic family. We also felt their tragedies.

We also acknowledge the assistance of Floreada Harmon and John Blunston of Jackson, Mississippi, for allowing us to "pick their brains" about the glory days of Church Street. Floreada Harmon, the wife of pharmacist George Harmon, did not live on Church Street during the early days. However, she was well aware of the many social activities, and she was an administrative employee at the historical Smith Robertson Elementary and Junior High School in the late 1940s. Floreada was also a co-worker of Gladys Noel Bates, the brave woman who sued the great State of Mississippi in the 1940s. John Blunston grew up on historic Farish Street and has been a resident of Jackson, Mississippi, all his life. He attended the public schools of Hind County and graduated from Jackson State College. John Blunston has an eidetic memory, commonly referred to as photographic memory, and is able to recall names, incidents and dates without any hesitation.

We affectionately acknowledge the assistance of Ruth Williams, who made available the pictures and documentation about her parents, Walter and Nellie Williams. Ruth's early adult life was on East Church Street, and her family was the epitome of high society during those early days. Thanks also to Gwendolyn Loper and Gwendolyn Chamblis for providing information about Doris Tharp Hall. Special thanks to Norma Alexander and Sannette Langston-Smith for helping edit the book, Selika Sweet for her support, Amanda Bradley for her support and patience and Denise Sweet Owens for her assistance in all phases of publishing this book.

Finally, we thank those persons who shared their memories of growing up on Church Street: Annie Rose Wheaton Walker, whose father was pastor of the United Central Methodist Church; Ruby Thames Bryant, whose childhood friend was Grace Sweet; Grace Weakly Lee, who was the daughter-in-law of hotel owner Edward Lee Sr.; Randall Pinkston, who is currently a national television newscaster; Elijah Slaughter, who recently died; and Charlotte Shinault-Coleman.

Introduction

Organized on March 1, 2011, Unicorn is a nonprofit literary club based in Jackson, Mississippi. *Church Street: The Sugar Hill of Jackson, Mississippi* is Unicorn's first project, but it will not be our last literary endeavor. In the early 1930s and late 1940s, phenomenal things happened on Church Street in Jackson, Mississippi. Nearly all of the city's Negro professionals resided on this street, and most of their wealth was centered on Church Street in homes on the hill. This street, which stretches just a few city blocks, was a haven for the elites. Amazingly, no one outside the inner city of Jackson knew of the unbelievable successes of the residents on Church Street.

Church Street, on a small scale, rivaled the good life Negroes were experiencing in the great cities of Chicago and New York as we in the South were reading about the good times in Harlem in the *Pittsburg Courier*, the *Chicago Defender* and *Ebony* magazine. Therefore, members of Unicorn agreed that *Church Street: The Sugar Hill of Jackson, Mississippi* would be an appropriate title for the book.

Furthermore, most African Americans are familiar with the term "Sugar Hill." They read about and saw the pictures of the glory days of "Sugar Hill" in Harlem, New York, and the lower part of 63rd Street in Chicago. Sugar Hill was the residential section north of 145th Street to 155th Street, between Amsterdam Avenue to the west and Edgecombe Avenue to the east. Notables such as Thurgood Marshall, W.E. DuBois, Aaron Douglas, Count Basie, Duke Ellington, Coleman Hawkins and Lena Horne resided on Edgecombe Avenue. Boxer Sugar Ray Robinson owned an entire block of businesses—all his buildings were painted pink, as was his convertible Cadillac. Among black Americans, Sugar Hill gained the reputation of being "heaven on earth"—a place where blacks from the South would have it made. In the lingo of the Harlem Renaissance period, "sugar" referred to money, the ticket to high-style living. Thus, Sugar Hill became the name of the uptown area where prosperous African Americans resided. Wealthier blacks settled in the area in the 1920s and '30s to enjoy a view of the "valley" that was then central Harlem. Some purchased town houses, while others rented apartments in one of the twelve-story or fourteen-story buildings. In summary, migration from the South for the sweet life in the North helped to create the Sugar Hills in Chicago and Harlem.

Research performed by members of Unicorn indicates inconsistencies in referring to people of color. In earlier times, people of color were called "Negroes." First, they were referred to as "three fifths" and later as "coloreds." In the early 1960s, people of color were referred to as "blacks" or "Afro Americans," but they are presently referred to as "African Americans." Unicorn members concluded that there was never an official documented classification for people of color. Furthermore, the word "Negro" is used in the English-speaking world to refer to a person of black ancestry or appearance regardless of whether he or she is actually of African descent. This usage was accepted as normal until the later civil rights movement.

During the civil rights movement of the 1950s and '60s, some African American leaders in the United States, most notably Malcolm X, objected to the word, preferring "black" because they associated the word Negro with the long history of slavery, segregation and discrimination that treated African Americans as second-class citizens or worse. The term "Negro" is now widely considered to be obsolete and is not commonly used. However, it is still used in some historical contexts, such as in the name of the United Negro College Fund and baseball's Negro League. In order to be politically correct, the term "African American" will be used in this book when referring to people of color.

The Purpose of Unicorn

The aim of this book is to help the current generation of young African American Jacksonians to understand and appreciate the achievements of their unsung forefathers of over seventy-five years ago. This is a period of time before *Brown vs. Board of Education* and the passage of the Civil Rights Bill of 1964—a time before African Americans held any elected or appointed positions in Jackson. This is the time when the only support unit for those great souls was the immediate family.

Unicorn was established for the purpose of encouraging young African Americans to read more and to consider a career in writing. Finally, *Church Street: The Sugar Hill of Jackson, Mississippi* accomplishes Unicorn's mission of reaching those young African Americans who appear to have lost their way in life. It appears that what used to be the exception in the past is now the norm—namely, a high rate of obesity, unbelievable dropout rates, record-breaking crime statistics and early parenthood. Our main goal is to get back to the good and wholesome life described in this book.

A Demographic Overview of Church Street

The history of Church Street begins in 1835 with Thomas E. Helm, a white male, donating an eighty-square-foot lot to Mount Helm Baptist Church, the first African American church in the city of Jackson. This lot was located in the northeast corner of Lot #1 in the old Cohea Lease near the Farish Street Historic District. Records at the Mississippi Department of Archives and History show that between 1895 and 1900, Mount Helm Baptist Church was identified as being located on the corner of Grayson and Church Streets. It is believed that the street became known as Church Street due to the presence of Mount Helm and the Farish Street Baptist Church.

General Characteristics

Church Street, two-fifths of a mile in length, is that stretch of street beginning in the west on Mill Street and ending in the east on Grayson Street, now known as Lamar Street. In Church Street's heyday, there were approximately nineteen houses on West Church and forty-seven houses on East Church, giving a total of sixty-five houses. Out of the sixty-five houses located on Church Street, approximately 11 percent were rental properties, while 89 percent were being lived in by the owners. Amazingly, over 50 percent of the homeowners were professional people.

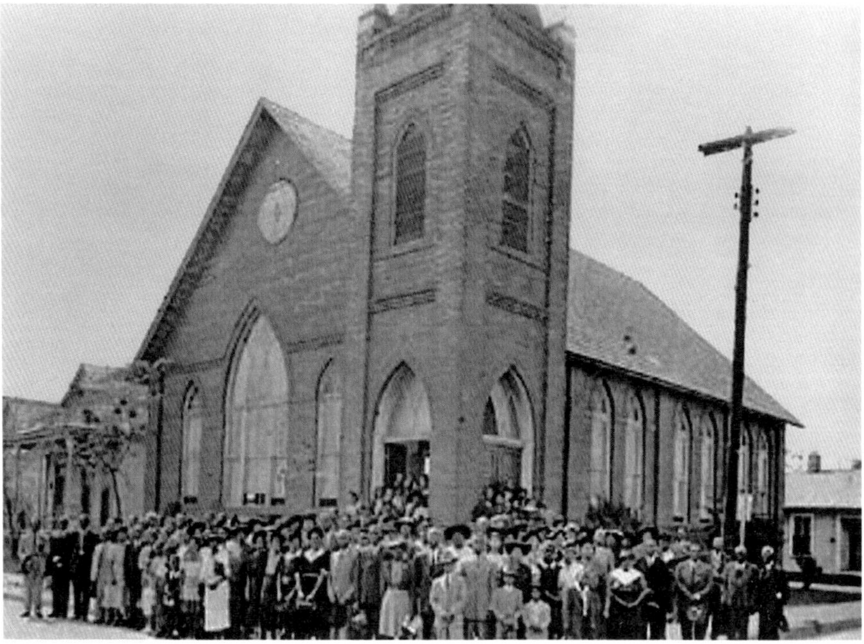

Farish Street Baptist Church.

Economic Characteristics

There were four businesses located on West Church Street. On the corner of Mill Street and West Church was the Mason Blacksmith Shop. Behind the blacksmith shop was the famous and nationally known Edward Lee Hotel. Several houses below the hotel, in front of Parker's Alley, was Moore's Beauty Shop and Beauty School. Behind Farish Street Baptist Church was Buster's Grocery and Market. Frank Conic's Superior Barber Shop was located on the corner of West Church and Farish Streets, opposite the Farish Street Baptist Church. On the corner of Farish Street and East Church was People/Gulledge Grocery. Immediately behind the grocery store on East Church was a row of ten shotgun-style rental houses owned by Crescent Laundry.

City of Jackson Quick Facts Comparison

The first African American church in Jackson was located on Church Street. In African American communities in the city, Church Street was the first street to be paved, the first with sidewalks and the first to offer garbage collection services. Church Street was also home to the first African American millionaire and the highest number of offspring attending college in any community—white or black—of its size.

Unit 1

Families

Chapter 1

The Mount Helm Baptist Church Family

The first family of Church Street is truly the church family of Mount Helm Baptist Church. The early days of Church Street begin with the establishment of Mount Helm Baptist Church. The congregation of Mount Helm Baptist Church, the oldest black Baptist church in the city of Jackson, had its beginning in the First Baptist Church of Jackson, Mississippi. The membership of First Baptist Church, organized in 1835, was made up of both blacks and whites. The slave members met in the basement with a white deacon present.

When slavery was abolished, blacks withdrew from the First Baptist Church at the request of its deacons. Without a building to worship in, the former slaves had to erect a church of their own. Thomas E. Helm, a white Presbyterian businessman, and his wife, Mary, gave them eighty square feet of property on what is now the corner of Lamar and Church Streets. Here, in 1868, the former First Baptist members built their first church, a wood-frame building that would stand for forty-two years. The Helms' gift also included money to assist with building the church. To show their appreciation and to honor their benefactors, the African Americans named their sanctuary Mount Helm Baptist Church. Reverend Marion Dunbar was the first pastor.

The first split of the Mount Helm membership came in 1893, when Reverend Elbert B. Topp, the second pastor, and a large number of Mount Helm's members left to form Farish Street Baptist Church. The underlying reasons for the split were disagreement and confusion over the state of the

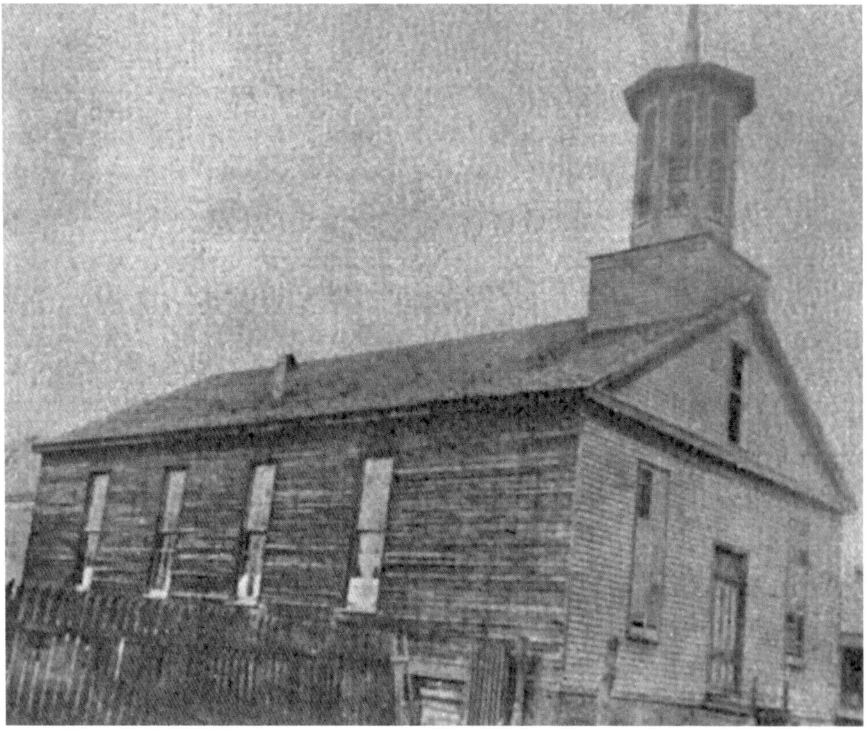

Mount Helm Baptist Church at the corner of Church and Grayson (now Lamar). *Photo by Ben Bradley.*

church's finances. Like Mount Helm Baptist Church, Farish Street Baptist Church played a major role in the lives of the inhabitants of Church Street. Farish Street Baptist Church is located on the corner of Farish Street and West Church Street. Reverend Topp lived on Church Street.

When Reverend Charles Price Jones became pastor of Mount Helm in 1895, the congregation was divided a second time. Reverend Jones proposed changing the name of Mount Helm to Church of Christ. After a lawsuit, Reverend Jones was asked to leave the church, at which point he started the Church of Christ (Holiness) U.S.A.

Reverend Adolph Lemuel Rice became the fifth pastor at Mount Helm. Also employed at Jackson Teacher's College, Reverend Rice lived in the church's parsonage, which was located where the current church sits. His diligence in enforcing the payment of pledges led to the loss of many members. Reverend Rice died in 1958, and Reverend Thomas B. Brown became the sixth pastor, serving from 1958 until 1979. The congregation

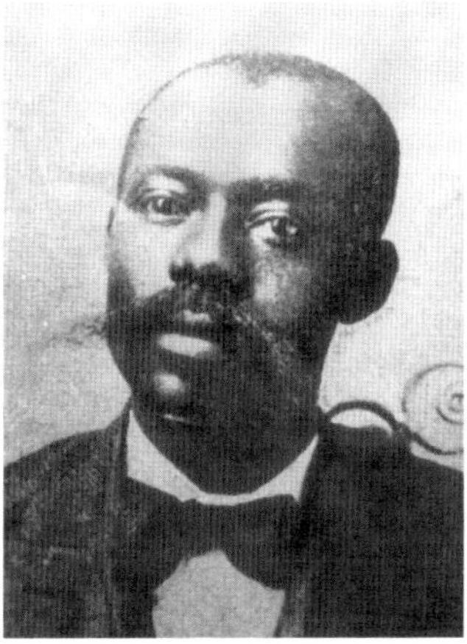

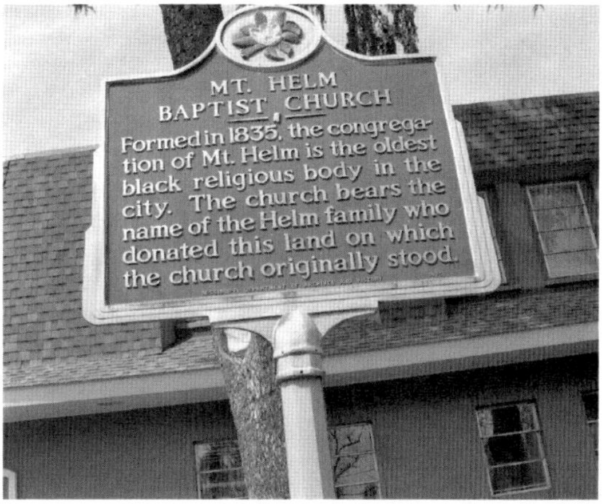

Above, left: Reverend Elbert B. Topp.

Above, right: Mount Helm Baptist Church has been located on Church Street throughout its entire 175-year existence. *Photo by Ben Bradley*.

truly loved Reverend T.B. Brown. Under his leadership, a new church was erected on the corner of Church and Dreyfus Streets.

Mount Helm has been the wellspring of several well-known churches in the Jackson area. Churches that were founded by former members of Mount Helm include:

Farish Street Baptist Church
Cade Chapel Baptist Church
Pearlie Grove Missionary Baptist Church
Mount Calvary Baptist Church (Tougaloo)
Koinonia Baptist Church
Church of Christ (Holiness) U.S.A.

The philosophy of Mount Helm Baptist has always been that of conservatism in religion. From its inception, Mount Helm has always required that its ministers be educated. In fact, the majority of its ministers have had college degrees. Even today, Mount Helm Baptist Church is the most conservative African American Baptist church in the bold city of Jackson—and maybe the most conservative in the entire state. Mount Helm has always stood steadfast to its principles. Moreover, it is truly unbelievable how Mount Helm's influence has made its way into many churches in the city of Jackson.

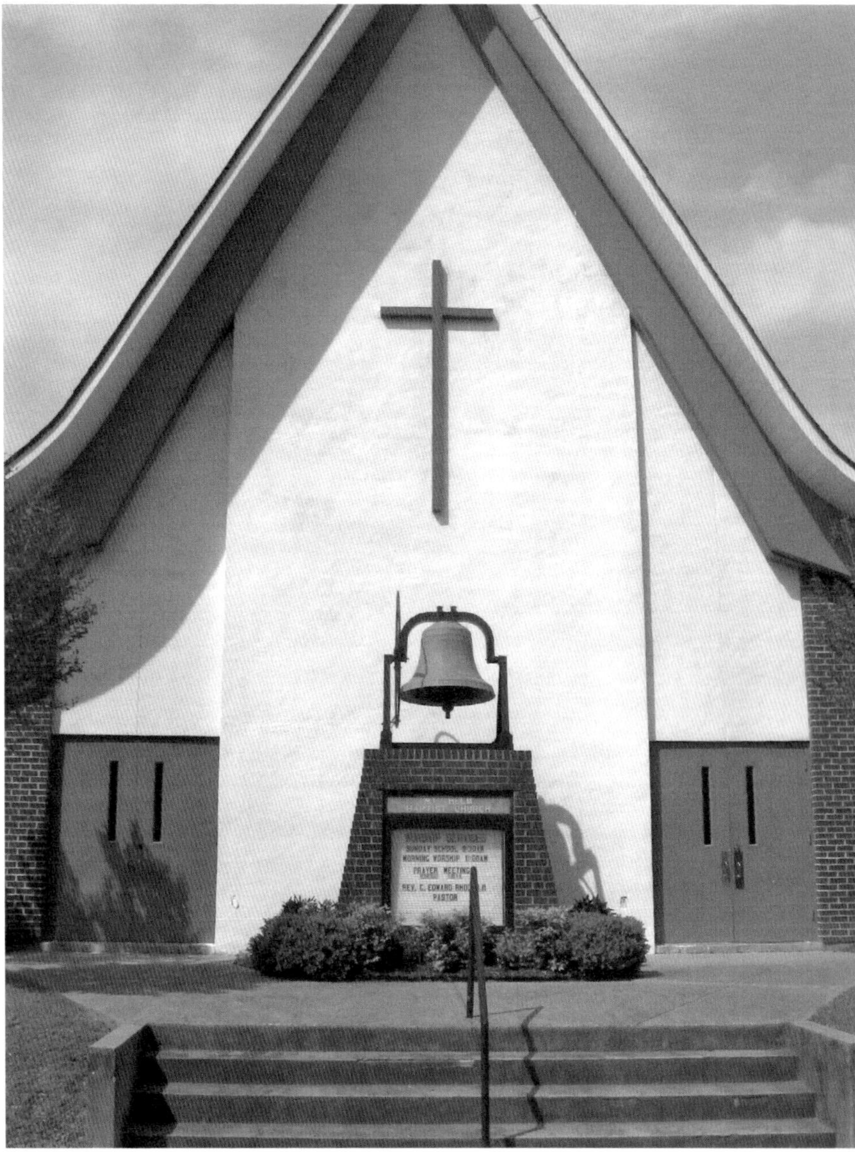

Mount Helm Baptist Church. *Photo by Ben Bradley.*

Bishop Charles Price Jones came from Selma, Alabama, to pastor the Mount Helm Baptist Church in Jackson in 1895 after declining the presidency of Alcorn College. When Mount Helm Baptist Church relieved Reverend Jones of his pastorship, he immediately established the Church

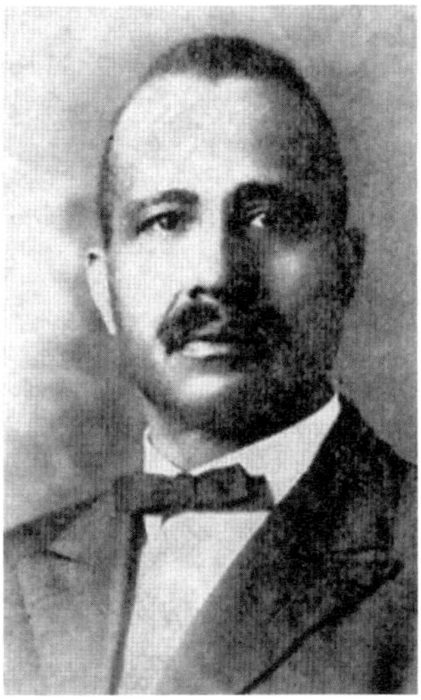

of Christ (Holiness) U.S.A. on the corner of Monument and Grayson Streets, a "stone's throw" from Mount Helm.

In 1897, Reverend Jones and Bishop Charles Harrison (C.H.) Mason of Memphis, Tennessee, combined their churches. In 1907, however, the two preachers dissolved the partnership due to differences in their interpretations of speaking in tongues. Mason's new church became known as the Church of God in Christ (COGIC). Reverend Jones remained on Monument Street in Jackson.

The Church of Christ (Holiness) U.S.A. went on to establish a college, the Christ

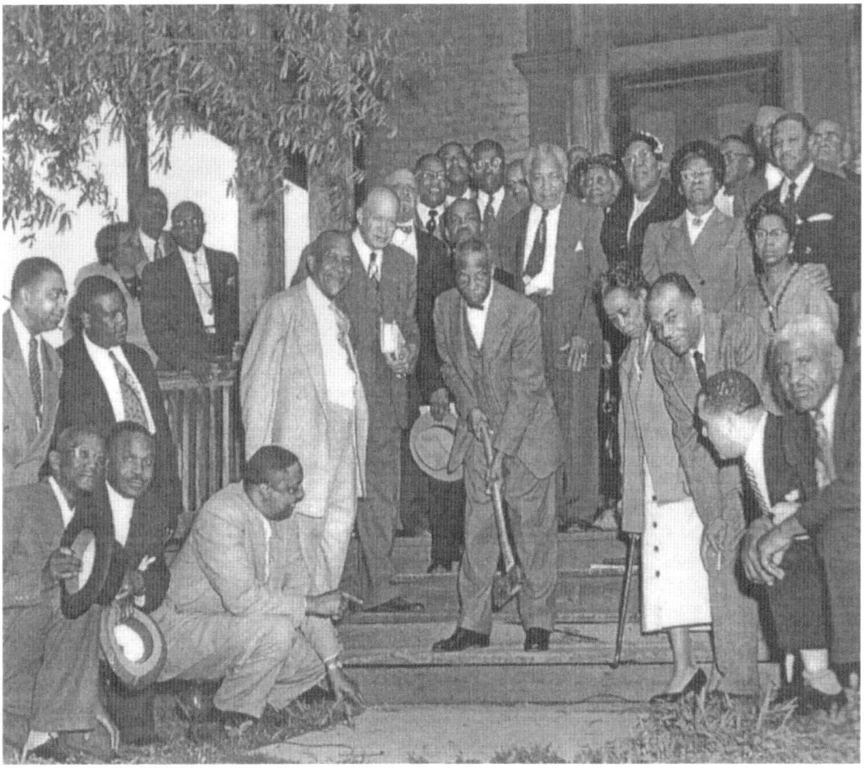

Top: Bishop Charles Price Jones.

Bottom: Bishop C.H. Mason (with axe) severed his ties with Bishop C.P. Jones of Jackson.

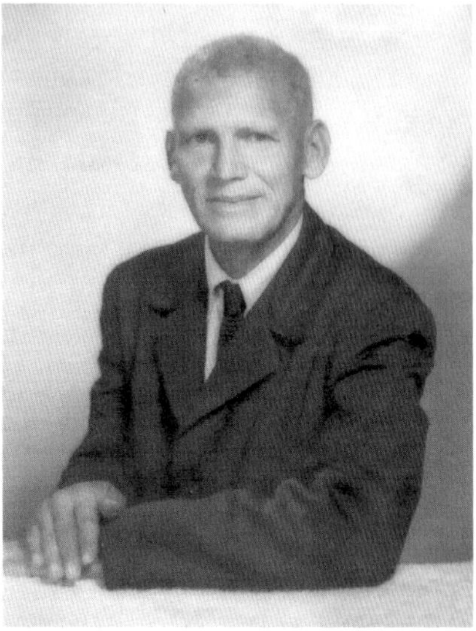

Ernest H. Slaughter.

Missionary and Industrial College (CMI), and Reverend Jones went on to write and publish over one thousand hymns. Presently, there are 154 churches and 14,000 members throughout the United States under the umbrella of Church of Christ (Holiness) U.S.A. Bishop Mason's organization, the Church of God in Christ (COGIC), has produced a large number of churches over the years. It is estimated that there are 5 million members throughout the world in twelve thousand churches.

For many years, the head deacon of Mount Helm was Ernest H. Slaughter, who was noted for giving prayers almost every Sunday. Mr. Slaughter lived in Tougaloo and had seven children, all of whom attended Mount Helm from infancy. As small children, all seven often fell asleep during services, stretching out across two or three pews until church was over. Mr. Slaughter brought his brood to church every Sunday in the old pickup, even during occasional Mississippi snowstorms, when no one else would be there but the Slaughter family.

Central Methodist Church Parsonage was also located on East Church Street. Reverend Wheaton lived there in the early 1940s. Reverend Holland also lived in this house. Reverend Wendell Taylor decided to move the parsonage to the Georgetown section of the city. The old structure appears to be in good shape even though it was built in 1895. In the early 1960s, the home was sold to a white-owned store, New Deal Grocery. It was then turned into a rooming house.

Following is a photograph of the home of Reverend Elbert Topp, the first minister of the Farish Street Baptist Church. The house, built in 1895, was located next door to the Central Methodist Church parsonage on Church Street. It was renovated in the 1950s by Reverend Topp's son and now serves as a rental house.

In the early days, five great African American ministers had homes on Church Street: Reverend Elbert Topp, Reverend A.L. Rice, Reverend

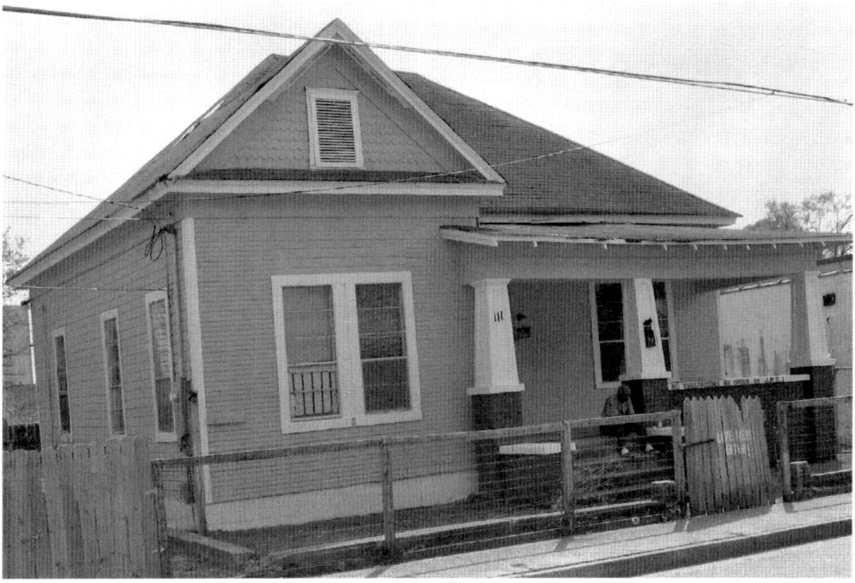

Above: Central Methodist Church parsonage, 2011. *Photo by Ben Bradley*.

Below: Reverend Topp's residence.

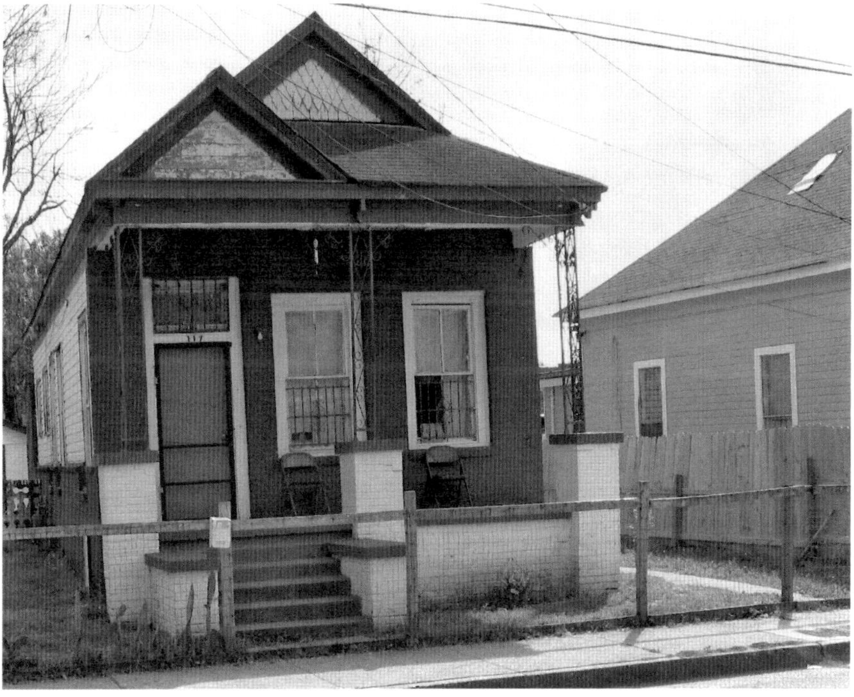

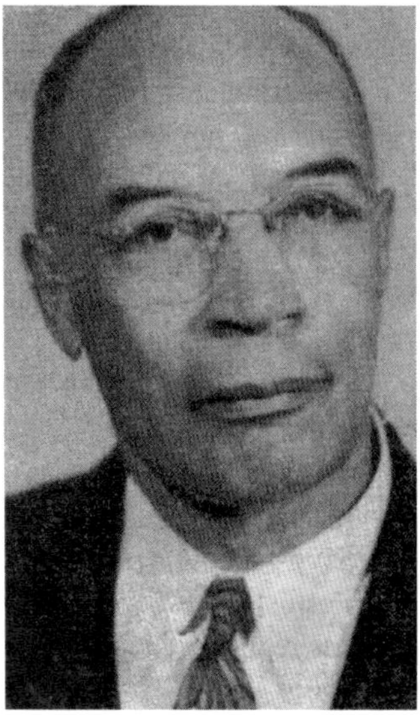

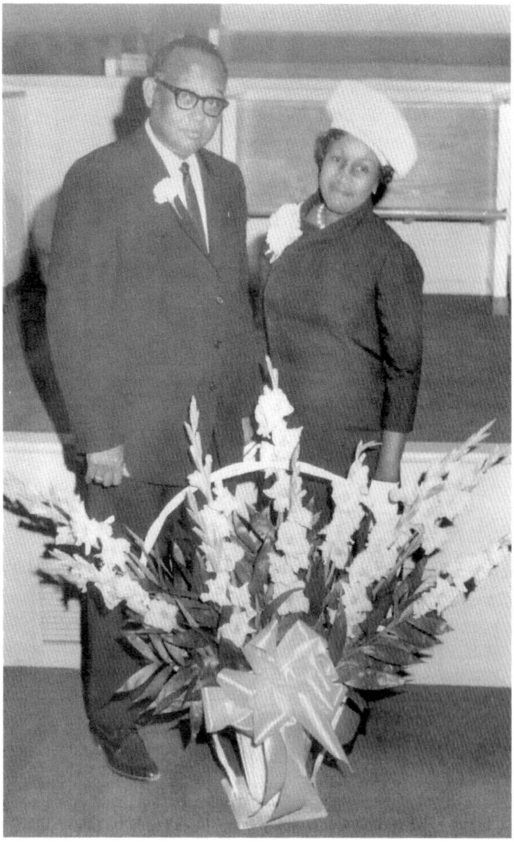

Above: Reverend A.L. Rice, pastor of Mount Helm during the 1930s.

Right: Reverend Thomas B. Brown with his wife. Reverend Brown was pastor at Mount Helm for twenty years.

Charles Price Jones (Mount Helm Church parsonage), Reverend James D. Wheaton and Reverend Holland.

The Reverend Elbert B. Topp served as pastor of Mount Helm Baptist Church from 1888 to 1893. Reverend Topp and 210 members of Mount Helm organized what is known today as Farish Street Baptist Church on the corner of Farish and Church Streets in the heart of the Farish Street Historic District. Reverend Dr. Hickman M. Johnson is the current pastor of Farish Street Baptist Church, having served the church since August 1968. From 1967 to 1968, Dr. Johnson also served as chaplain of Tougaloo College.

Reverend Thomas B. Brown served as the sixth pastor of Mount Helm Baptist Church. He served without any problems for twenty-one years. He died while still pastor of Mount Helm.

Like Reverend Rice, Reverend Brown had a second job. He was dean and later president of the Mississippi Baptist Seminary. Although Reverend Brown had a spotless record at Mount Helm Baptist Church, his tenure at the seminary was tainted. Through discrepancies in the record books, it was discovered that GI students (veterans) were paying some instructors to mark them as present during hours in which they were not actually in attendance. The GIs were required to reimburse the U.S. government for all discrepancies found by the federal auditors.

Although Reverend Brown was not personally involved, the incident occurred under his watch. Soon thereafter, Reverend Brown had a freak accident, falling from a ladder while repairing his house. This accident would eventually lead to his death. Many believe that Reverend Brown grieved himself into an early grave because of the scandal at the seminary.

Chapter 2

The Redmond Family

The most influential person of the early days of Church Street was Sidney Dellon Redmond of Jackson, who lived at 221 East Church Street. Dellon was born in Ebenezer, Mississippi, on October 11, 1871, to former slaves and attended Rust College after completing high school in Ebenezer. He graduated from Rust College in 1893. Later, he attended Illinois Medical College (IMC), graduating in 1897. After graduating from IMC, he attended Howard University for postgraduate courses. He practiced as a physician and surgeon for a number of years until his health deteriorated, forcing him to retire. Thereafter, Dr. Redmond studied law, becoming a practicing lawyer in 1910.

Dr. Redmond's first wife was Ida Revels, the daughter of Hiram R. Revels, a United States Senator from Mississippi. Hiram Revels succeeded Jefferson Davis in the Senate after Davis resigned to accept the presidency of the Confederacy. Revels also resigned from the Senate a few years later to become the first African American president of Alcorn A&M College in Alcorn, Mississippi.

The union of Dr. Redmond and Ida Revels bore two children: Ester Redmond Austin (Chicago, Illinois) and attorney Sidney Revels Redmond (St. Louis, Missouri). Mrs. Ida Revels Redmond died in 1914. Dr. Redmond later married Johnnie Grace King of La Grange, Georgia, granddaughter of the late Senator Horace H. King of Alabama. To this union were born Ruth and Linnie. Linnie died during her childhood. Ruth went to college, married and lived the remainder of her life in Washington, D.C.

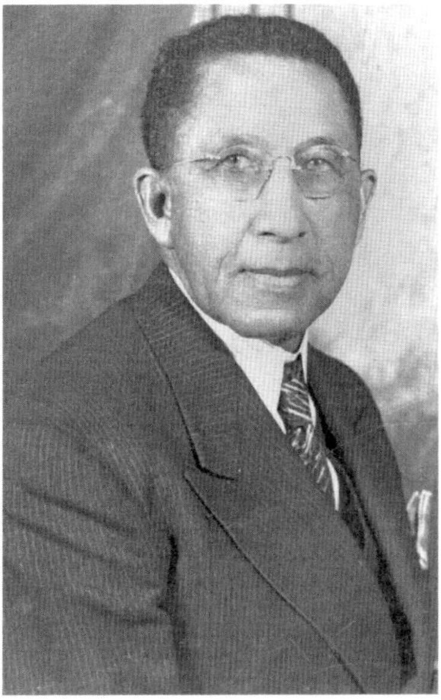

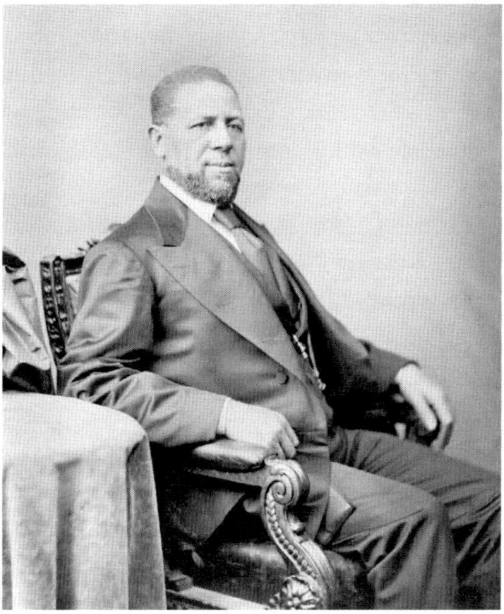

Above, left: Dr. Sidney Dellon Redmond. *Courtesy of Smith Robertson Museum & Cultural Center, Jackson, Mississippi.*

Above, right: Hiram R. Revels. *Library of Congress.*

Dr. Sidney Redmond joined Perry Howard in his law practice in Jackson and in Washington, D.C. Dr. Redmond was disbarred in 1915 and reinstated in 1920. In 1926, his son joined him in the practice of law. In 1929, Perry Howard and Dr. Redmond were charged with selling federal jobs. Both men received acquittals and continued working with the Black and Tan Republican Party.

The Honorable Perry Howard was head of Jackson's Black and Tan Republican Party, which consisted of an African American faction of the Republican Party, with headquarters located on North Farish Street at the corner of Oakley Street.

Dr. Redmond was a medical doctor, a brilliant lawyer and an outstanding businessman. Arguably, he was the first African American millionaire in America. At one point in the 1930s, Dr. Redmond owned more than three hundred rental houses in Jackson. He owned property in the 100 block of Farish Street where the McCoy Building is now located, as well as houses on Redmond Avenue and Revels Street in the Virden Addition area. He also owned houses in west Jackson, near Jackson State College in Redmond Alley. Additionally, Dr. Redmond owned a drugstore at the corner of Capitol and

Farish Streets. He was also president of a black-owned bank on South Farish Street and a principal stockholder in four city banks owned by whites. The last building constructed by the Redmond family is located on North Farish Street, directly in front of Central Methodist Church, where the Big Apple Inn is housed.

Sidney Dellon Redmond and, later, his son Sidney Revels Redmond were the biggest property owners on Farish Street. Sidney Revels is presently in charge of the Redmond estate, which was valued at $356,000 at the time of Dr. Redmond's death.

Sidney Revels Redmond attended the public school (Smith Robertson) in Jackson until his mother died. He was in the seventh grade at that time. He then attended Tougaloo prep school and graduated from Talladega High School. He went on to graduate from Rust College and Harvard Law School. At the time that Sidney Revels Redmond attended Harvard, there were only twenty-five African Americans attending the university. After he became a lawyer, Redmond practiced law in Jackson for two years. Probably because

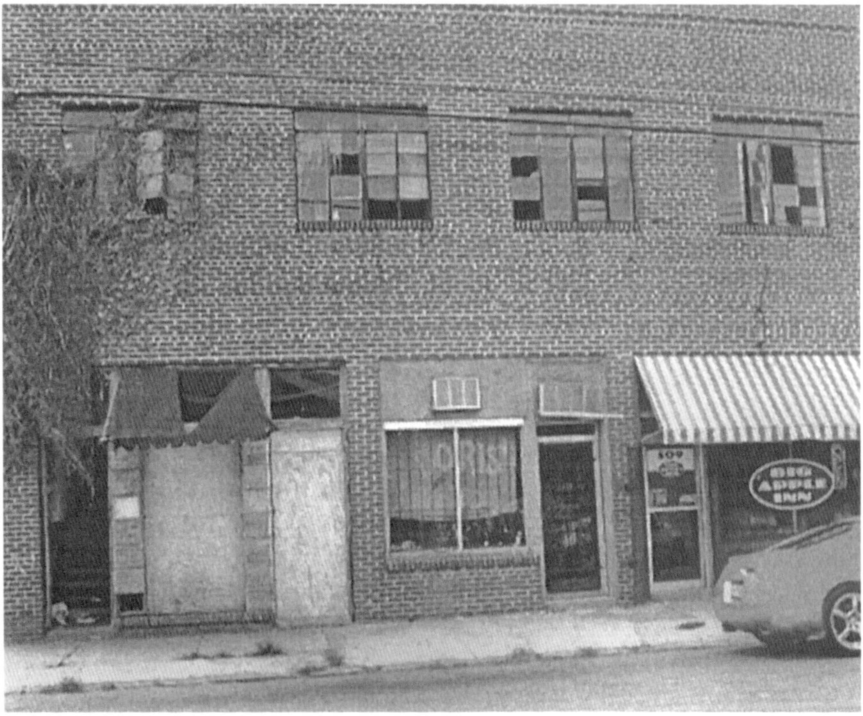

The Big Apple Inn, the last building constructed by Dr. Redmond. *Photo by Ben Bradley.*

he joined his father's law firm at a time when his father and Howard were being prosecuted, he felt the practice of law in Mississippi too hostile, so in 1929, he moved to Illinois for a short time and then to St. Louis, Missouri, later becoming president of the National Bar Association, which was the national organization of African American attorneys. He became affiliated with the NAACP and worked with Walter White. He also united with the Republican Party.

Dr. Sidney Dellon Redmond was not only the most prominent person on Church Street; he was also the most prominent African American in the city of Jackson. News articles about Dr. Redmond appeared weekly in the *Mississippi Enterprise*, the *Jackson Advocate*, the *Clarion-Ledger* and the *Jackson Daily News*. Also, Charles H. Wilson, principal of Smith Robertson Junior High School, wrote a book about the life of Dr. Sidney Dellon Redmond. This book, entitled *God! Make Me A Man*, was written in the late '40s and published in 1950.

Dr. Redmond employed a full-time maid, yard man and chauffeur at his Church Street home. He also employed Lewis Perkins as a full-time plumber. Dr. Redmond donated a fire truck and street sweeper to the City of Jackson. Although Dr. Redmond had a chauffeur, he walked to and from his office each day from Church Street to the 100 block of Farish Street to maintain his health. Like most of the residents of Church Street, Dr. Redmond's children attended college. Dr. Sidney Dellon Redmond died in 1948, leaving one of the largest African American estates in the South.

Dr. Sidney Dellon Redmond and Dr. A.H. McCoy, a popular dentist, were good friends. Although Dr. Redmond owned property all over the city of Jackson, he elected to rent office space in Dr. McCoy's building located at 115 North Farish Street. Attorney W.L. Mhoon also had an office in this building.

The two good friends entered into several business ventures together. Dr. Redmond and Dr. McCoy were the inventors of several arrestors and insulators that would keep torpedoes from exploding when striking a ship. Our research was unable to uncover if these inventions were actually used by the U.S. Navy. The two men also organized and established the Carver Veteran Trade School for returning African American World War II veterans who were eligible for the GI bill. The GI bill played a major role in the decline of Church Street (this will be explained in another chapter).

Dr. Redmond motivated and trained young African Americans who wanted to become lawyers in Jackson. Percy Greene was one such young man. Greene was a good friend of Dr. Redmond's son, who was attending

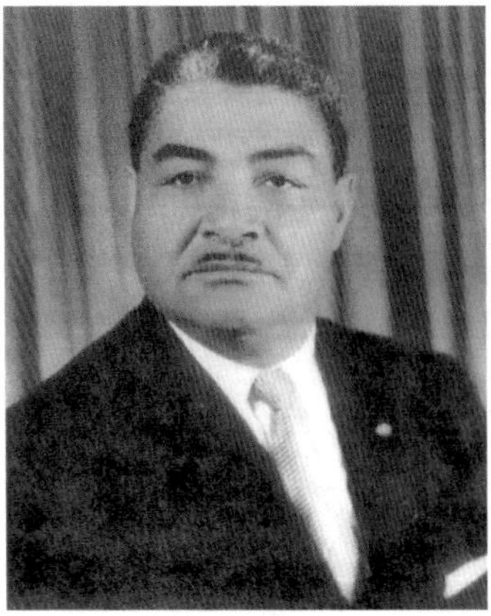

Left: Percy Greene.

Below: Dr. McCoy's multi-floor building at 115 North Farish Street housed Dr. McCoy's dental office, Beadle's studio, Dr. Redmond's office and the Blackstone Café.

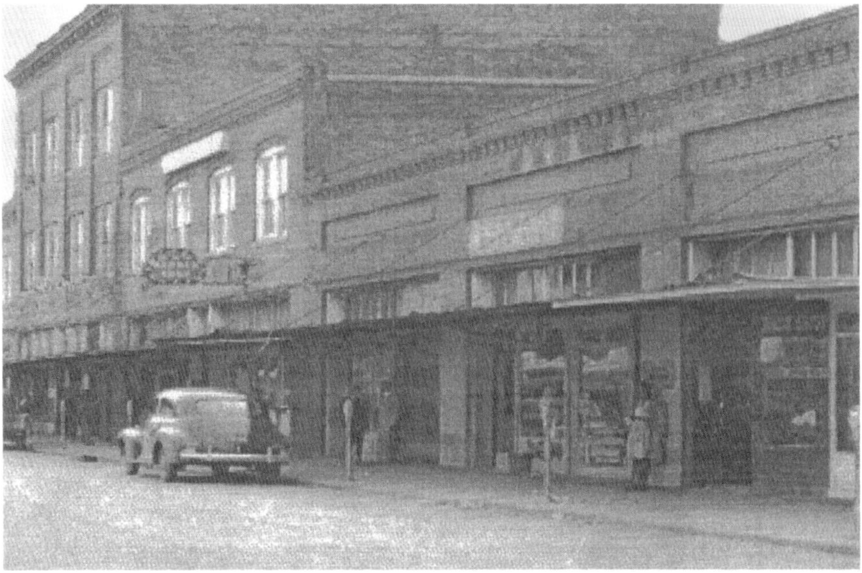

Harvard University at the time. Percy Greene wanted to become a lawyer by "reading the law." A person "reading the law" was someone who had not attended law school but could take the bar exam after reading law under a judge or practicing attorney for an extended period of time. The State of Mississippi, at that time, required two years.

Percy Greene was engaged by Dr. Redmond as a law clerk for nearly four years. In 1926, he took the Mississippi Bar Exam and failed. In 1926, he again took the exam, but this time his name was missing from the results. Prior to taking the bar exam a second time, Percy had had an altercation with a white man in the capitol building. Realizing that passing the bar was now out of the question, Percy was encouraged by Dr. Redmond to consider journalism. Percy Greene, a Jackson College graduate, eventually became the editor and owner of the *Jackson Advocate*, the oldest African American newspaper in Mississippi.

In 1941, several of Dr. Redmond's professional friends appeared in articles in local newspapers when Mrs. Annie E. Mhoon, wife of attorney W.L. Mhoon, sued Dr. A.H. McCoy for slander and sought $10,000 in damages for an article written in Percy Greene's *Jackson Advocate* newspaper on January 11. Mrs. Mhoon felt that the article was libelous against her reputation. The first trial ended with a verdict against Mrs. Mhoon; however, she convinced the judge to set aside the verdict and grant a new trial. Our research failed to establish the outcome of the second trial.

Dr. Sidney Dellon Redmond of 223 East Church Street touched the lives of many Americans, and especially the professional African Americans. His reputation as a lawyer extended from his home on the hill of Church Street to the White House in Washington, D.C. Dr. Redmond was a physician and a lawyer, as well as an astute businessman. He and attorney Perry Howard were also seasoned politicians. Without these two gentlemen, the Black and Tan Republican Party would have died much earlier in history than it did.

While on official business in Jackson in January 1942, Brigadier General B.O. Davis stayed at Dr. Redmond's home on East Church Street. The general was in town to discuss the topic of "World War II and the Negro" with the African American leaders in Jackson. Professors O.B. Cobbins and I.S. Sanders were invited to Dr. Redmond's home to attend this meeting. General B.O. Davis was the first African American to achieve the rank of brigadier general in the segregated United States Army. General Davis's son was a colonel in the segregated U.S. Army and later attained the rank of general.

In 1943, Dr. Redmond was honored in the "International Who's Who in America." He was the only Negro in that 1943 edition.

On May 23, 1943, Dr. Redmond sponsored an oratorical contest. Each participant spoke on the same subject: "How to Improve the Economic Status of the Negro." Students from local colleges participated, and a grand prize of $200.00 was awarded to the top speaker.

The date was February 14, 1948, and the headlines in the *Jackson Advocate* read in part, "Dr. S.D. Redmond Is Dead." The story about Dr. Redmond's death appeared in all the newspapers and magazines, including *Jet* magazine. The *Jackson Advocate* featured the story for two weeks. The funeral was held at the Central United Methodist Church on historic North Farish Street, and Reverend James D. Wheaton was the officiating minister. Dr. Redmond's

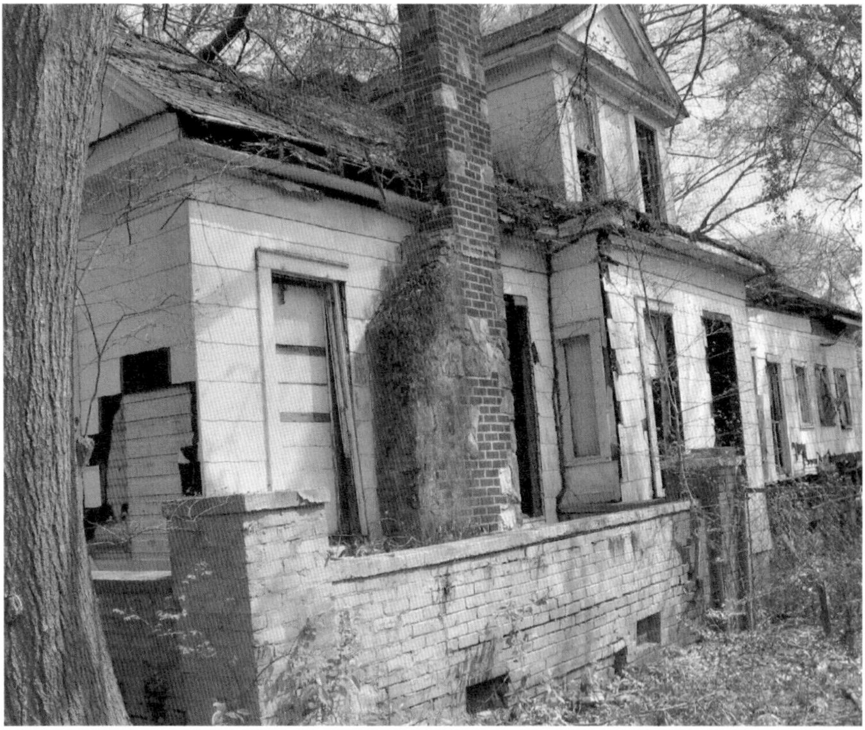

The Redmond home in decline.

funeral was more than a tradition ceremony—it was an event. A veritable "who's who" of the African American community was in attendance, and several distinguished gentlemen were selected to do the eulogy, which began with remarks by Reverend W.A. Bender of Tougaloo College. Following is a list of pallbearers, both active and honorary:

Active Pallbearers:

David D. Shepherd (Shepherd Kitchenette)
Frank W. Washington
Burr Brown (realtor)
McKenzie Coleman
Dorsey Williams
Wiley Spence

Honorary Pallbearers:

S.L. Green (president of Campbell College)
Jacob L. Reddix (president of Jackson College)
Attorney W.L. Mhoon
Dr. G.A. Price
Dr. E.W. Johnson
Dr. C.L. Barnes
Dr. A.H. McCoy
Dr. A.M. Hall
Dr. C.H. Christian of Jefferson Memorial Hospital (Negro hospital)
Dr. R.O. Williams
Dr. M.F. Atwood
Dr. W.E. Miller
Dr. L.B. Stewart
Dr. O.F. Smith of the Sallie Harris Clinic (Negro hospital)
Dr. LeRoy A. Smith

Mrs. Johnnie Redmond, widow of Dr. Sidney D. Redmond and reputedly one of the nation's wealthiest Negro women, died of a liver ailment at the St. Dominic Hospital in Jackson at the age of seventy-one. The St. Dominic Hospital was located on the corner of President and Amite Streets. In later years, the hospital relocated to a multimillion-dollar facility located on Highway 25 (Lakeland Drive) near Highway 55.

Chapter 3

The Britton/Perkins Family

The legacy of the Britton family in Jackson had its beginning at 234 East Church Street in the home of the Perkins family.

Lewis Perkins, the patriarch of the Perkins family, was a man of many talents. He served in the U.S. Army in World War I and once pitched a baseball game against the legendary Satchel Paige. He was later employed by the aforementioned Dr. Sidney Dellon Redmond as a full-time plumber.

The Perkins house on Church Street was always open to family members. At one time, Lewis Perkins; his mother, Rachel Perkins; and his sisters, Lucinda Smith, Amanda Collier, Rebecca Clay and Elizabeth Perkins, all lived in the home located at 234 East Church Street. Lucinda's husband was a bellhop at the famous King Edward Hotel. Sisters Mary and Elizabeth attended Campbell College.

In 1918, Reverend A.B. Britton Sr. married Mary Perkins, a teacher. Reverend Britton owned a 365-acre farm in Shubuta, Mississippi, that was uniquely sharecropped by a white man. Mary Perkins Britton gave birth to six children: Louis, Albert, Rachel, Morris, Lucille and Grace. She died in the Methodist Parsonage in Shubuta in March 1932 shortly after giving birth to Grace.

Reverend A.B. Britton Sr. then took Grace, the youngest child, to Jackson to live with her uncle Lewis Perkins and her aunts at 234 East Church Street. Albert Britton Jr. came to Jackson to live with the Perkins family at age fourteen. The remainder of the Britton family moved to the farm in Wayne County. Reverend Britton made funds available for the education of his two

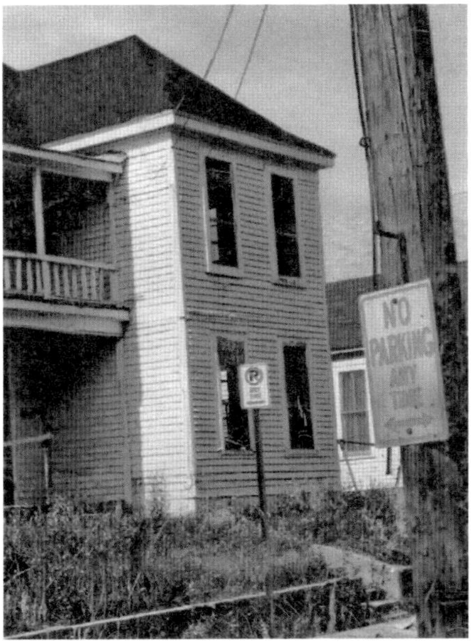

Left: The home of Lewis Perkins. *Photo by Ben Bradley*.

Below: Members of the Perkins/Britton family outside their home.

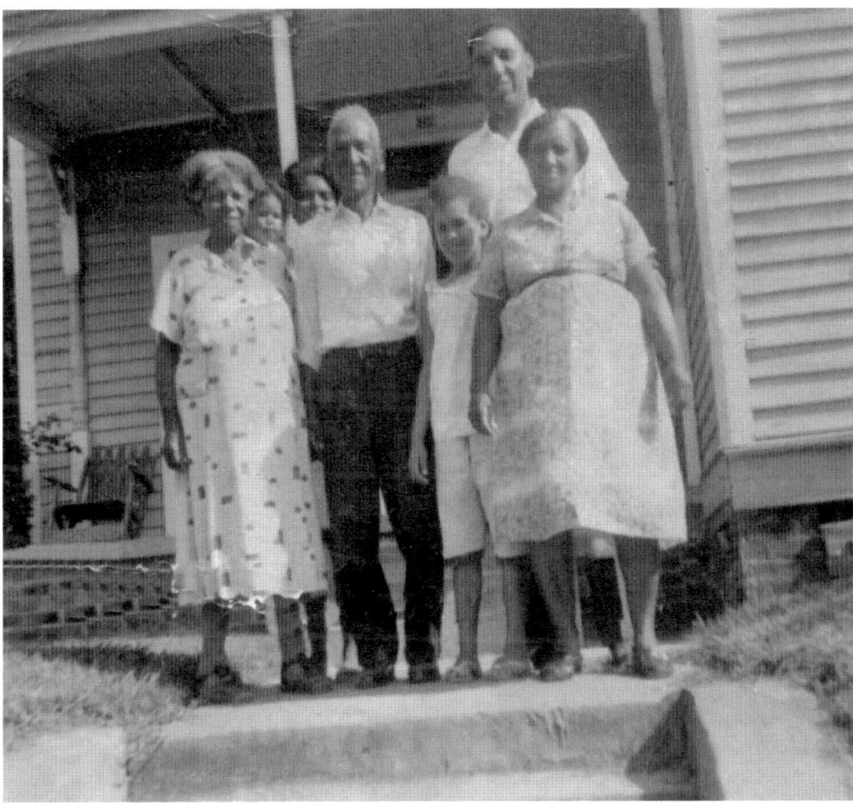

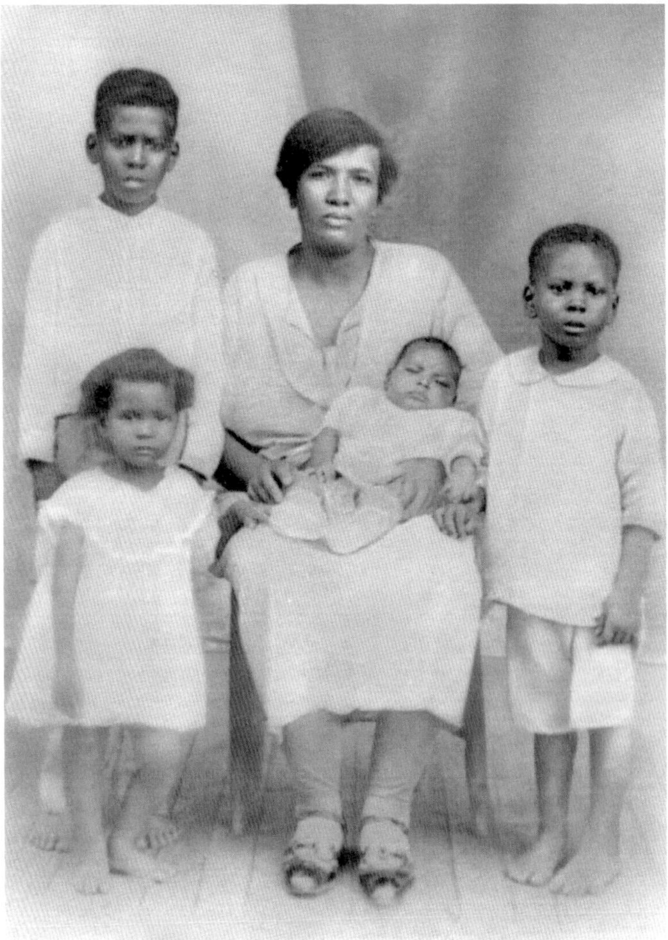

Mary Perkins Britton with her children. Albert Britton Jr. stands at the far right.

children now living in Jackson. Like most of the residents of Church Street, he strongly believed in educating his children.

Grace Britton attended the Lutheran School, spent one year at Smith Robertson Junior High School and graduated from Lanier High School. Albert Britton Jr. attended Lanier High School and graduated in 1939. He was both student body president and valedictorian of his class. While in high school, Albert worked odd jobs with his uncle and played football and drove a cab during the summer months for his brother James Britton, who lived in Laurel, Mississippi.

A.B. BRITTON JR.

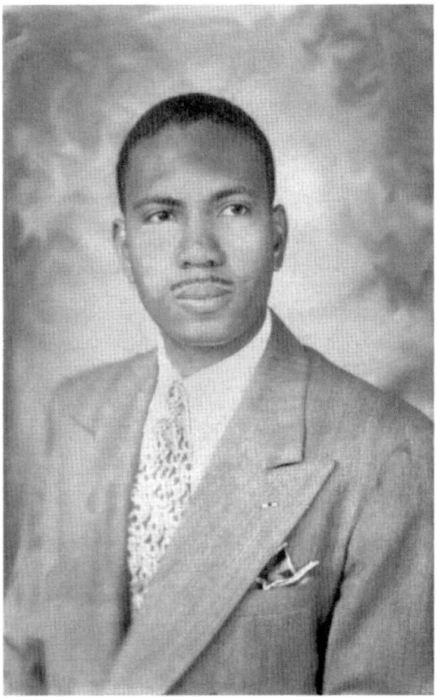

A.B. Britton Jr. at twenty-three.

A.B. Britton Jr. attended Tougaloo College and graduated within three years. He also played on the school's football team. His education continued at Howard University's College of Medicine, where he obtained his degree in 1947. His medical internship was completed at Freedman Hospital in Washington, D.C., and his work in obstetrics and gynecology was completed at Flynt Goodridge Hospital in New Orleans, Louisiana.

Education and public service were paramount in Dr. Britton's life, yet he still found time to come to the aid of his country in both World War II and the Korean War. This he also did with distinction, earning the Bronze Star for excellent medical service while in the armed forces. Dr. Britton made another tremendous mark in the medical field by participating in the first clinical trials of penicillin shots at Fort McClellan, Alabama, in 1944.

Dr. Albert B. Britton Jr. eventually purchased a building at 527 North Farish Street and set up his practice, which lasted sixty-four years. He also purchased a home on West Church Street behind the Farish Street Baptist Church.

It is ironic that Dr. Britton's Medical Arts Building was located next to the lot on which the Sallie Harris Clinic once stood. The Sallie Harris Clinic was one of the two hospitals owned by African Americans. The other clinic was Jefferson Memorial Hospital, which was owned by Dr. C.B. Christian. There was a time during the early days of Church Street that African American doctors were not allowed to practice medicine in white-owned hospitals such as Charity Hospital (later renamed University Hospital), Baptist Hospital and even St. Dominic Hospital.

Dr. A.B. Britton Jr. was the first African American physician admitted to the staff of Baptist Hospital in Jackson. This was a major achievement for the young physician from West Church Street, as the Baptist Hospital was considered the cream of the crop for hospitals—and for white folks.

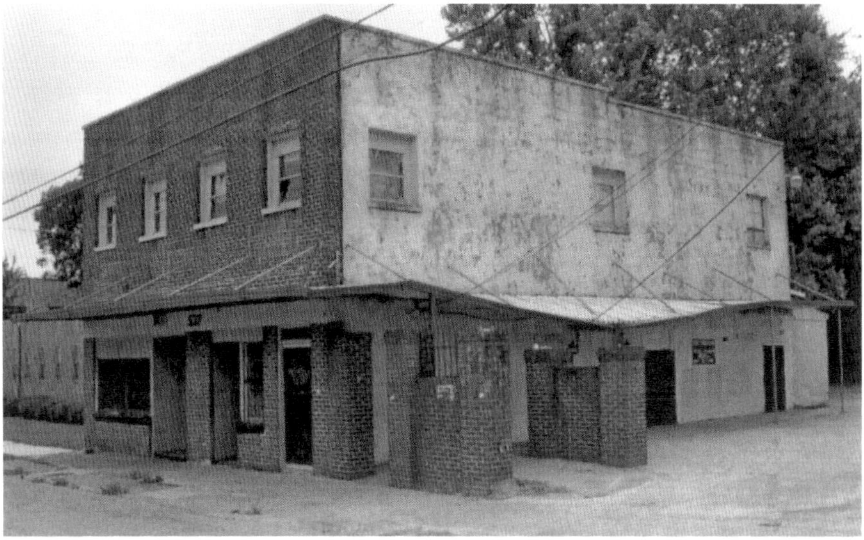

Dr. Albert Britton Jr.'s medical building at 527 North Farish Street.

President Dwight D. Eisenhower appointed Dr. Britton to the Mississippi Advisory Committee to the U.S. Commission on Civil Rights. Dr. Britton testified about the denial of African American voting rights at a hearing before the commission when it convened in Jackson in 1964. He also met with Martin Luther King Jr., Stokely Carmichael, Charles Evers, James Farmer and Jim Foreman to finalize the Mississippi Freedom March.

Two African Americans and three white persons were sworn in as members of the committee, which worked with the U.S. Commission on Civil Rights on racial complaints: Dr. A.B. Britton Jr., an African American physician of Jackson; retired U.S. Navy admiral Robert Briscoe of Liberty; James Lucius Allen, an African American druggist of Columbus; the Reverend Murray Cox of Gulfport, committee chairman; and Mrs. Jane M. Schutt, president of the Mississippi United Church Women. Later, in 1965, the committee was expanded to seven members, and Dr. Britton was appointed chairman.

As Dr. Britton continued breaking down barriers, he became the target of the Mississippi State Sovereignty Commission. He was referred to as having long been associated with belligerent movements, and his every move was spied upon by the Sovereignty Commission. Sadly, some of the personnel spying on Dr. Britton were members of his own race. Despite all this, he was never deterred from his duties as chairman of the Mississippi Advisory Committee to the U.S. Commission on Civil Rights.

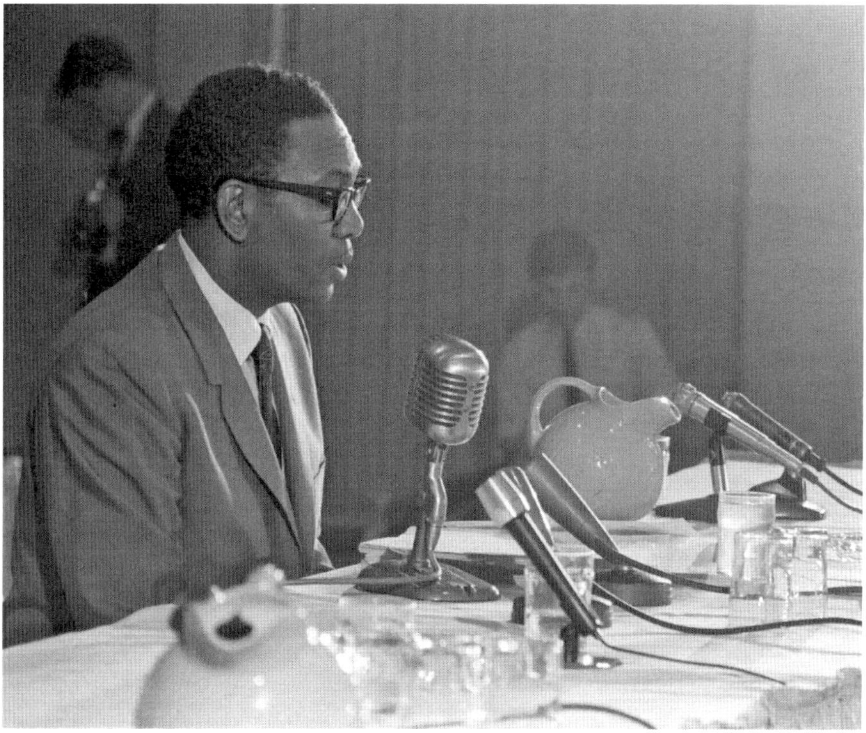

Dr. Albert B. Britton speaking at a hearing of the Senate Subcommittee on Employment, Manpower and Poverty at the Heidelberg Hotel in Jackson, Mississippi. *Courtesy of the Jim Peppler Southern Courier Photograph Collection at the Alabama Department of Archives and History.*

The following information about Dr. A.B. Britton Jr. was found in the Sovereignty Commission records:

> *February 29, 1960*
> *Memo to: File*
> *From: Zack J. Van Landingham*
> *Subject: Civil Rights Advisory Committee, Mississippi*
>
> *At 8:15 p.m. on February 26, 1960, my telephone at my residence at 4231 Athens Drive rang, and when my wife answered the telephone, the caller asked to speak to Mr. Van Landingham. I went to the phone, and the caller asked, "Is this Mr. Van Landingham?" I said yes. He then said, "Listen carefully to what I have to say. I can't tell you my*

name. There is going to be an attempt made tonight on the life of Dr. Britton." The caller immediately hung up the phone.

Dr. A.B. Britton Jr. is the Negro physician who was appointed a member of the Civil Rights Advisory Committee for the State of Mississippi. According to the telephone directory, his residence is 1510 Whitfield Mill Road, telephone FL 5-3051. His office address is 527 North Farish, telephone Fl 3-0997.

Upon receiving the above-mentioned telephone call, I immediately attempted to contact Chief of Detectives M.B. Pierce at his residence, but the phone was busy. I then telephoned the Police Department and talked to Captain of Detectives Bennett. I informed him of the telephone call and suggested that he immediately get in touch with Chief of Detectives Pierce to determine what action the police were going to take.

I then telephoned Attorney General Joe Patterson at his home and informed him of the above telephone message and also told him I had immediately contacted the police. Mr. Patterson stated that he believed that was all that could be done. He was of the opinion that it was possibly some crank calling.

Chief of Detectives Pierce then telephoned the writer at my residence. We discussed the message. I told him I was sure from the tone of voice that it was some white man calling rather than a Negro. The man talked very distinctly and did not appear to be under influence of liquor, nor was I able to discern anything out of the ordinary in his tone of conversation. Chief Pierce stated that ordinarily on receiving anonymous messages such as this, the Police Department did nothing. However, on this occasion, he finally decided he would have a patrol car watch the residence and also some detectives placed in the vicinity to also keep a watch on the residence of Dr. Britton. It was decided that possibly it would be best not to notify Dr. Britton of the call, inasmuch as he would possibly notify the papers and possibly notify the Civil Rights Commission in Washington to the effect that he was being intimidated here in Mississippi. Chief Pierce requested that I inform him should any other calls be received in this regard.

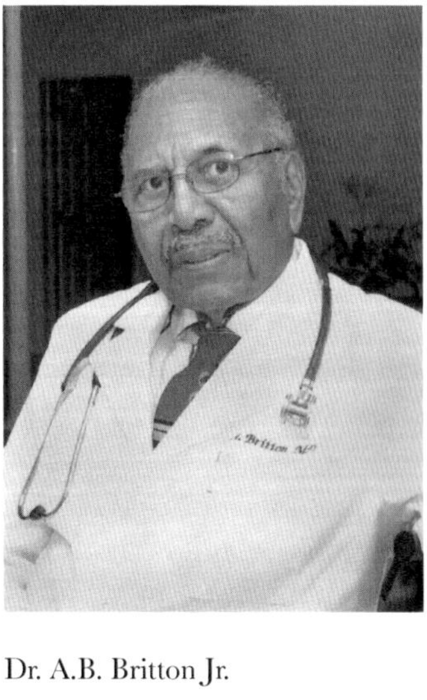

Dr. A.B. Britton Jr.

On the morning of Saturday, February 27, 1960, I talked with Chief Pierce, and he advised me that nothing happened during the night around the residence of Dr. Britton.

Dr. A.B. Britton Jr. died at the age of eighty-eight. His illustrious career was artistically summarized in his obituary:

It was no accident or stroke of luck that Dr. Albert Bazaar Britton Jr. was the first African American physician admitted to the staff of Baptist Hospital in Jackson, Mississippi. The life he began in Enterprise, Mississippi, in 1922 and continued on West Church Street would lead to the pursuit of excellence in medicine, securing equality for all through civil rights and working to enhance our community through service. During the Civil Rights Era, Dr. Britton used his knowledge and influences to help make a difference for so many in Mississippi and around the nation. Dr. Britton was a Charter Member of the Mississippi Health Services Agency and served as its secretary, vice-president and president, as well as being a member of its Board of Directors. He was co-director of the Nurse Midwifery program of the University of Mississippi Medical Center and director of the County Health Improvement Program at UMMC.

As a result of the shooting of a sixteen-year-old girl in Moss Point in 1964, Dr. Britton headed a committee of the National Medical Association and Medical Committee for Human Rights to provide emergency medical treatment for civil rights workers coming to Mississippi. In its resolution, the association recognized that it was likely the volunteers participating in the sit-in and mass demonstrations would incur bodily injury, and they did. As a result of Dr. Britton and the Medical Association, these civil rights workers were assured medical treatment.

To make sure that future generations of African Americans were able to pursue medical careers, Dr. Britton directed the federally funded Medical Preceptorship Program for black medical students, both in Mississippi and out of state. Dr. Britton's 1969 testimony before the U.S. Senate led to permanent changes to the health care delivery system in Mississippi and studies of the rates of poverty and hunger among its residents. These efforts were also noticed nationally. Dr. Britton served the National Medical Association as a member of the board of directors and vice-president. The organization recognized his work by honoring him as the General Practitioner of the Year.

The honors, awards and professional achievements mentioned here barely scratch the surface of who Dr. Albert Bazaar Britton Jr. was. The best testimony comes from the thousands of babies he delivered and families he cared for. In fact, his greatest gift might be the sixty-four years he spent as a general practitioner with a specialty in obstetrics and gynecology at 527 ½ North Farish Street in Jackson, Mississippi.

Dr. Britton's contributions to the medical profession, his struggle for civil rights and work in the armed forces ensure that although he is no longer with us, his legacy will live on.

GRACE BRITTON SWEET

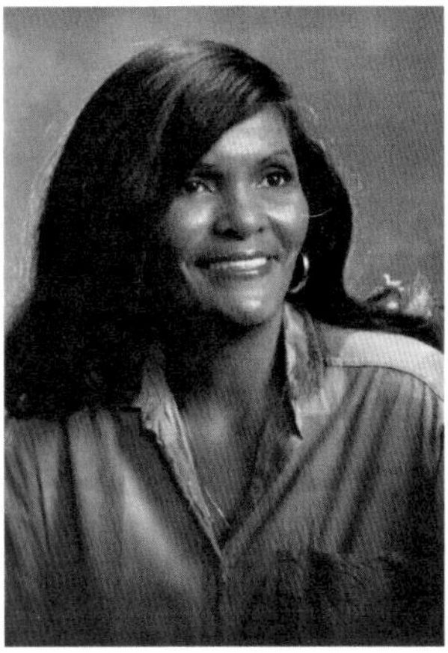

Grace Britton Sweet.

The Britton legacy continues with Grace Britton, who attended the Lutheran School on Blair Street, Smith Robertson Junior High School on Bloom Street for a short period of time and in 1948 graduated from Lanier High School on Ash Street. Like her brother, Grace Britton attended and graduated from Tougaloo College, and like her mother, Mary Perkins Britton, Grace Britton became a teacher and educator. Grace had no choice but to obtain her college degree, as her father, Reverend A.B. Britton Sr., was a strong believer in education and instilled the need for an education in the minds and hearts of his children.

Grace Britton met Dennis Sweet Jr. in July 1952. They were married on December 21, 1952, and their wedding was the first to be held at Christ the King Catholic Church on Lynch Street. This union produced three children, two of whom went on to become lawyers and the other a physician. One of the lawyers is currently a sitting judge in Jackson. The other lawyer was voted one of the top seven lawyers in the United States in 2003. Grace Britton Sweet's commitment to education is also evidenced by her grandchildren, four of whom are lawyers and one a physician. The two younger grandchildren are pre-med majors, while two more are hoping to attend law school. Grace Britton Sweet spent many years in the classroom as a concerned teacher and counselor. Recently retired, she became the matriarch of the Sweet family and is on the job 24/7.

Tougaloo College best summed up Grace Britton Sweet's career as an educator when she was awarded the Meritorious Leadership Award. Her citation reads as follows:

> *Few people embody the spirit of service and the dedication to community, the enduring value of tradition and the foresight to preserve Mississippi's cultural heritage for future generations that characterize Tougaloo College more so than Tougaloo's own Grace Britton Sweet. This gentle woman has accomplished great deeds and has unselfishly reached back to strengthen the quality of life for many others.*
>
> *With this citation, Tougaloo College gratefully acknowledges your years of superior professional leadership as Director of Alumni Affairs and your spectacular success in having the Medgar Evers Community declared a Historic Area and in having the Medgar Evers home donated to Tougaloo College.*
>
> *Tougaloo College recognizes your outstanding service to the Jackson community and the State of Mississippi as one of the first three black teachers to integrate the Jackson Public School System. The programs you designed to assist high-risk students in the public schools, to prevent dropouts and help to end the cycle of drug use and despair among Mississippi's youth remains an enduring pattern of inspiration and success.*
>
> *One among her many gifts is the understanding that the investment in education, the growth of character and the concern for worthy values requires the tireless stewardship of teachers and counselors in Mississippi's public schools. Her legacy as one of Tougaloo's most capable ambassadors of tradition, culture and learning shall not soon be surpassed.*
>
> *Well-deserved recognition and gratitude are due this generous community servant, practitioner of strong values and tender vision, mentor, mother and friend. Tougaloo College proudly bestows upon Grace Britton Sweet, on the occasion of its 133rd Commencement Exercises, the Meritorious Leadership Award.*

For almost sixty years, Grace Britton Sweet has had the right to vote. She can vividly recall the day she registered. As an African American woman living in the South, she was one of only a few black Americans who had the right to cast a ballot as early as 1953. In states such as Alabama, literacy tests were given as a way to bar African Americans from voting.

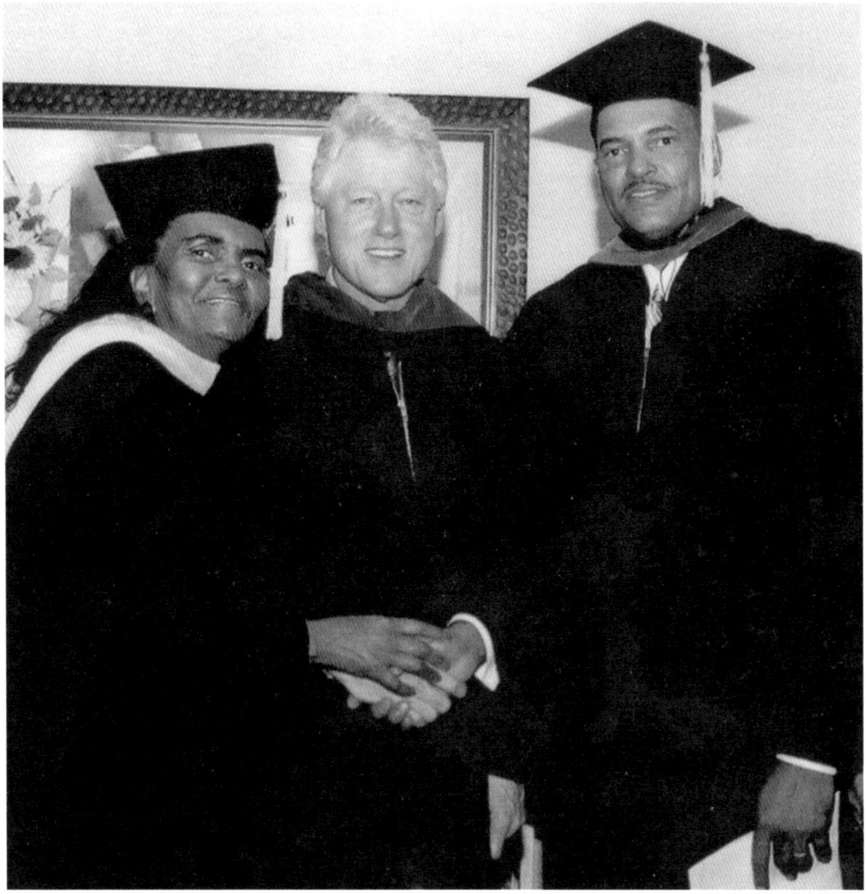

Grace and Dennis Sweet with Bill Clinton.

Grace had to travel out of the state of Mississippi to receive her master's degree because as an African American, she could not attend the white universities that offered graduate degrees. In 1959, she attended the University of Wyoming, where she made all As. She and her husband, Dennis, were offered employment in the school system there but decided to return to Jackson. Grace completed her master's degree in biology from Southern University and A&M College in Baton Rouge, Louisiana. Even after receiving her degree, Jackson Public Schools refused to pay her for the degree because it was not in education. It took the president of Southern University to intervene so that she would receive her raise of approximately $2,000 for the year.

Even though Grace had the opportunity to leave Jackson, she and her husband saw Mississippi as their home and were willing to deal with the adversity that existed in the Jim Crow South. So they traveled during the summers sometimes with the children while Dennis attended the University of Mines and Metallurgy in Raleigh, Missouri, and Atlanta University in Atlanta, Georgia.

Grace is glad she made sacrifices in this manner and put an emphasis on her children's education. She emphasized to her children what her father told his children about the answer to breaking the cycle of oppression: it is through an education, land ownership, voting and money.

Chapter 4

The Hodge Family

Claude Hodge and his wife, Georgia, lived at 203 East Church in the white cottage on the southeast corner of Bloom Street. The old home was torn down in the early 1960s to make a right-of-way for High Street, which extended from the corner of Monument Street and Farish Street across East Church Street.

Church Street, in its heyday, was the apex of professional and economic life for African Americans, and the Hodge family was no exception. Claude Hodge, a realtor, businessman and a cement finisher, was born in 1881. His father, Eli Hodges, was born into slavery, and his mother was Rebecca Seffield. Georgia Hodge was a housewife that attended to their rental property. The Hodges were members of Central United Methodist Church.

While Mr. Hodge was securing rental properties and building the Crystal Palace building, Mrs. Hodge, with her beautiful sun hat, gloves and long flora-print dresses, was busy working in her flower garden that covered the front and back yards. Mrs. Hodge would often entertain her female friends using her fine china and silverware. Mrs. Hodge always wanted to travel and visit the Bellingrath Gardens in Mobile. However, this desire was never achieved because Mr. Hodge died and she was propelled into being the head of the family, the astute businesswoman and the savvy realtor.

Claude Hodge built the Crystal Palace building in 1930. This sturdy, two-story building still stands at 540 North Farish Street. The Crystal Palace Ballroom, a big ballroom with a stage located in the far left corner and a

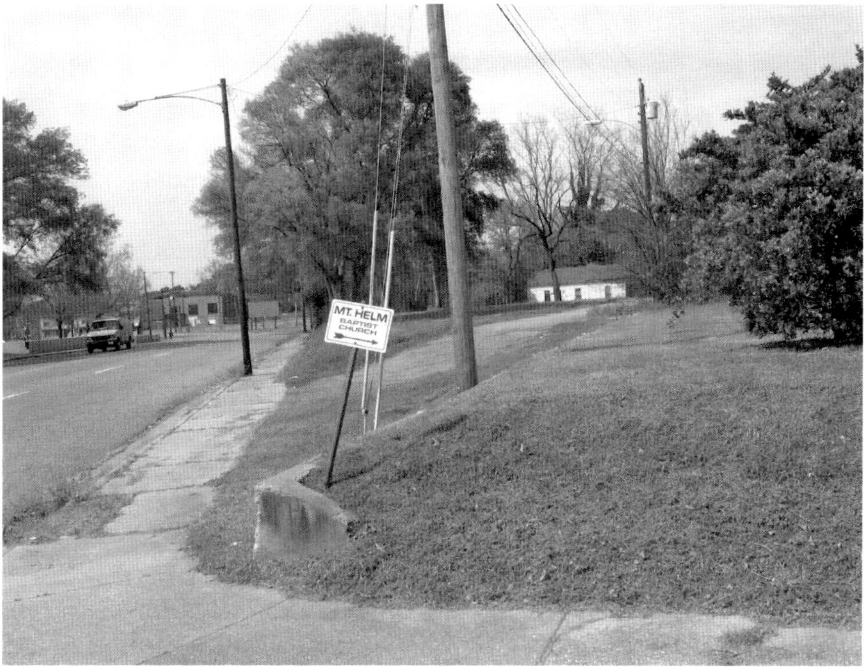

Above: Site of the Hodge home.

Below: The Crystal Palace.

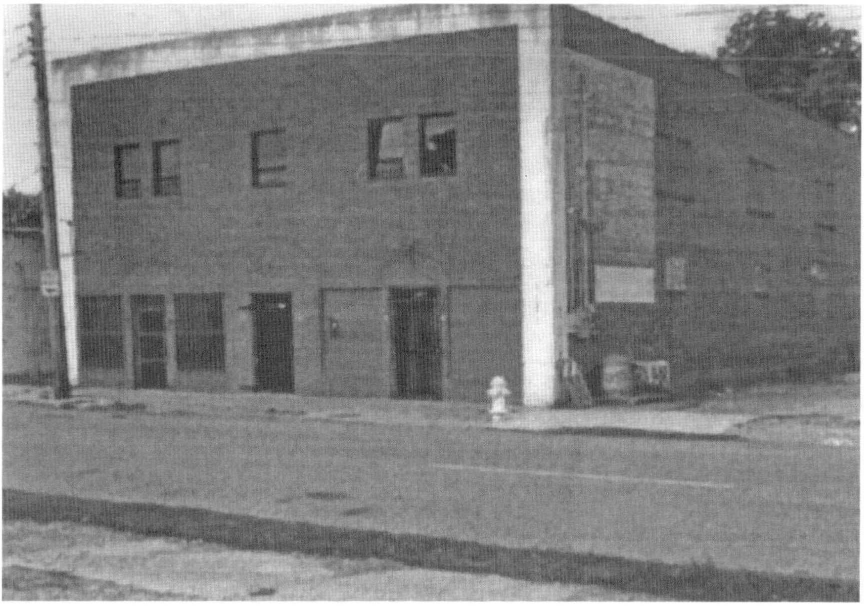

spacious dance floor, occupied the second floor of the building. A chandelier filled with beautiful crystal lights hung from the ceiling. The Crystal Palace was the most celebrated nightspot on Farish Street during the 1930s and early '40s, and its upstairs ballroom hosted entertainers such as Duke Ellington, Cab Calloway, Louis Armstrong, "Papa" Celestin, Jimmie Lunsford, Andy Kirk, Fletcher Henderson, Count Basie and Fats Waller.

The Crystal Palace Ballroom came into prominence because many of the big bands played there and many social affairs were held there. These affairs were well attended by the young elites of Jackson. The Crystal Palace Ballroom was the place where the African American elites could meet and greet in their fine clothes.

Poet Margaret Walker Alexander celebrated the nightclub in the poem "Crystal Palace" in her collection *Farish Street Green*. Alexander described the club as "a place of elegance where 'bougie' black folks came to shoot a game of pool" and listened to down-home music. In 1968, Alexander founded the Institute for the Study of History, Life, and Culture of Black People (Margaret Walker Alexander National Research Center). Among her more popular works are her poem "For My People" and her 1966 novel *Jubilee*.

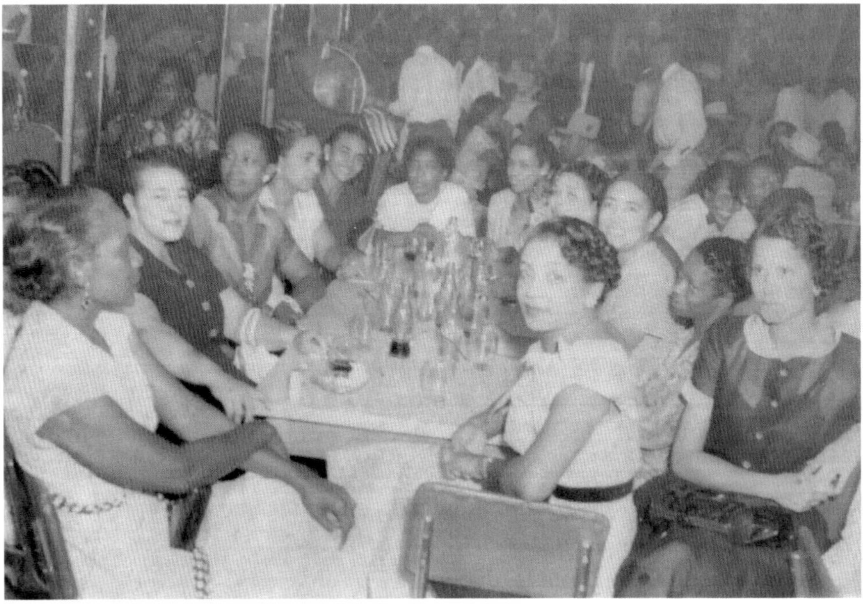

A Ladies Social Club meeting at the Crystal Palace.

Between 1930 and 1940, stories about the Crystal Palace Ballroom appeared in both the *Jackson Advocate* and the *Mississippi Enterprise* newspapers on a weekly basis. Editor Percy Greene would feature social news item in his "Up and Down Farish Street" column, while editor Sarah Harvey Stevens would write similar articles in her "Around Town" column. In 2010, the *Jackson Free Press* featured a detailed story about the famous Crystal Palace Ballroom in its magazine. Finally, author Bill Minor included a story about the Crystal Palace Ballroom in his book *Eyes on Mississippi*.

In the late 1940s, the Crystal Palace Ballroom's luster began to dim as several other businesses competed for the entertainment that drew large crowds to Farish Street. Among these businesses were the Blue Flame, operated by Joe Kitchen; the skating rink owned by Willie Miller; and Stevens Rose Room, owned by Willie Stevens. Even the Alamo Theater had live entertainment shows, including a performance by Nat King Cole. Claude Hodge did not live to witness the decline of his business, as he died on May 19, 1940, at age fifty-nine.

By late 1942, the Crystal Palace had been transformed into a USO service club. The USO was founded in 1941 in response to a request from President Franklin D. Roosevelt to provide morale and recreational services to U.S. uniformed military personnel. Roosevelt was elected as its honorary chairman. This request brought together several civilian organizations. Locally, the first director of the USO Club was Mr. C.B. Russell. He was later replaced by Thelma Saddle, who became very popular among the African American elites of the city.

The USO Club closed at the end of World War II, and the second floor of the Crystal Palace was transformed into several offices. Reverend Wilcher opened Wilcher's Music and Book Store, which was later owned and operated by Louis Marshall as Marshall's Book and Music Store for forty-six years.

The social club known as the Cavalier Club rented space on the south side of the building. Members of that club included Curtis Coward, Charlie Hughes, Louis Wade Wansley, Alex Norwood, James Fizer and brothers James, Joel and Paul Rundles.

Attorney Carsie Hall had an office in the building, as did the NAACP Legal Defense Fund, which was headed by attorney Marian Wright Edelman. Attorney Edelman played a major role in the development of the careers of Reuben V. Anderson, Fred L. Banks and Mel Leventhal and gained national recognition for her work with the Save the Children organization. Reuben V. Anderson and Fred L. Banks became judges. Mel

Leventhal married Alice Walker, the author of *The Color Purple*. Theirs was the first interracial marriage in the state of Mississippi. Mel became a great advocate for civil rights and was also regarded as a top-notch attorney. There is a lot of African American history within the walls of the "second floor" of the Crystal Palace building.

On the first floor, Claude Hodge's Crystal Palace building was divided into two sections separated by the stairways that led to the second floor and the Crystal Palace Ballroom. Dr. Lindsey opened a drugstore on one side, and Mr. Wilson opened a pool hall on the other side. Dr. Lindsey met an untimely death on Grayson Street (now known as Lamar) at the hands of an unknown assailant. Dr. Alston became the second operator of a drugstore in the Crystal Palace building. Years later, Edward Lee, owner of the Edward Lee Hotel and the Mill and Oakley Café, took over the pool hall that was previously operated by Mr. Wilson. When Dr. Alston decided to construct his own building in the up-and-coming area known as Virden Addition in 1951, Harmon opened his drugstore in the Crystal Palace. It remained there until 2003, when Harmon's Drug Store relocated to its present location at 614 North Farish Street.

Today, the Crystal Palace building is owned by the family of the late Dr. A.H. McCoy, and there is only one tenant, the Birdland Café, which is operated by Charlie Hughes.

The Hodge family of 203 East Church Street may not have been as outgoing as the Redmond family or the Conic family of Church Street, but they certainly made a significant impact. Claude Hodge was an astute businessman and had a vision that made him wealthy. Between 1940 and 1950, Georgia Hodge was, without a doubt, the most influential African American female in the city of Jackson.

Chapter 5

The Williams Family

Nellie Burbridge and Walter H. "Duke" Williams met at Tougaloo College, where they were both employed. Nellie was from New Orleans, Louisiana, and Duke was from Gurden, Arkansas. They arrived in Jackson in the late 1930s and taught at Tougaloo College for a number of years. Duke was the head coach of all of the sports, including football, basketball and baseball, as well as a professor of biology. He was known across the state for his winning teams. Nellie taught English and history at the Daniel Hand School at Tougaloo.

Duke's dream of starting his own life insurance company was born during a most difficult economic time in the United States because of the Great Depression, but with persistence and the support of a large family and friends, Security Life Insurance Company was launched. It was the first African American insurance company to be domiciled in Mississippi. Duke invited two of his out-of-town friends—Victor Jones and Edward Lipscomb—to move to Mississippi to become part of his new management team. With their assistance, the team recruited agents and stockholders for the company. The insurance business grew, and soon Duke had offices across the state, from the Delta to the Gulf Coast.

During this same time, Duke and Nellie acquired the Johnson School of Business, located at 603 North Farish Street. The school was housed on the second floor of the building owned by Dr. R.O. Williams, who also lived on East Church Street. The business school catered to veterans returning from the Korean War who desired the skills needed to run their own businesses, as well as young women who wanted to become secretaries. For about five years, Nellie managed and taught at the school with two other teachers. Unfortunately, the small school was closed after it was decided that it could not compete with Jackson College's business and secretarial programs.

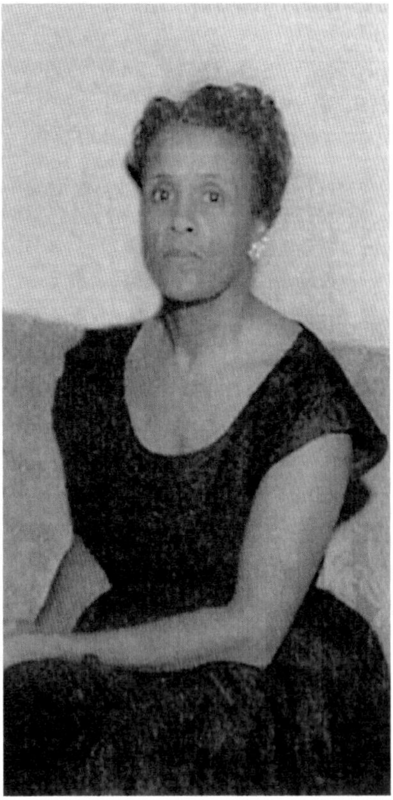

Nellie Williams.

After the school closed, Duke and Nellie invested in the Penguin Drive-In on Lynch Street with two friends from across the state. The Williamses bought out the partners and became the sole owners in the mid-1950s. The restaurant/café was located in west Jackson, across from the home of the president of Jackson College, Dr. Jacob Reddix. In the beginning, the Penguin had carhops as well as inside seating. It was known across the city as the place to buy barbecue, hamburgers and hot dogs. In the mid-1950s, the insurance company moved to Lynch Street, one block from the Penguin. The Williamses purchased that building from the Black Teachers Association. During the early years, the Williamses also had several other businesses, including an ice cream shop, a vending company and an upscale steakhouse. These businesses were short lived. However, this was not the case for the renamed Penguin Café, which fed generations of college and high school kids with the "Penguin Special"—two hot dogs with French fries covered with a special sauce—which became known as the "Joe Dyson Special" to the kids in the Washington Addition area. In Jackson, Joe Dyson was considered a celebrity. His band was one of the most popular in Jackson. He was at the Penguin almost every day, and he practically lived off the hot dog special. It may have had something to do with the price—thirty-six cents—which remained unchanged for eight years.

The Williams children attended private schools in the Jackson area. The sons attended the Daniel Hand School at Tougaloo College, Jackson College

Laboratory School and Tougaloo College High School. The daughter, Ruth, also attended the Jackson College Laboratory School and Holy Ghost High School. After graduating from high school, all three children went to college. Walter attended Talladega College in Alabama, Byron attended Tennessee State University and graduated from North Carolina College in Durham and Ruth attended Talladega College and graduated from Millsaps College. She was the first African American graduate of Millsaps.

Walter went on to medical school at Meharry Medical College in Nashville, Tennessee. He joined the U.S. Air Force as a medical doctor, and when he finished his tour of duty, he moved to Jackson to establish a practice. All of this was happening during the civil rights movement, and when Medgar Evers was killed, Walter's family encouraged him to move to Texas, where his wife, Barbara Thornton, had grown up in Fort Worth. Walter practiced medicine in Fort Worth until his death in the late 1990s. Walter and Barbara had two children: Lisa and Walter Jr.

Byron Williams followed in his father's footsteps and went into the insurance business. He worked in North Carolina and Missouri for several years before returning to Jackson to work with his father at Security Life until his death in the mid-1980s. Byron married Martha Davis of Jackson and had three sons: Byron Jr., Darryl and Perry.

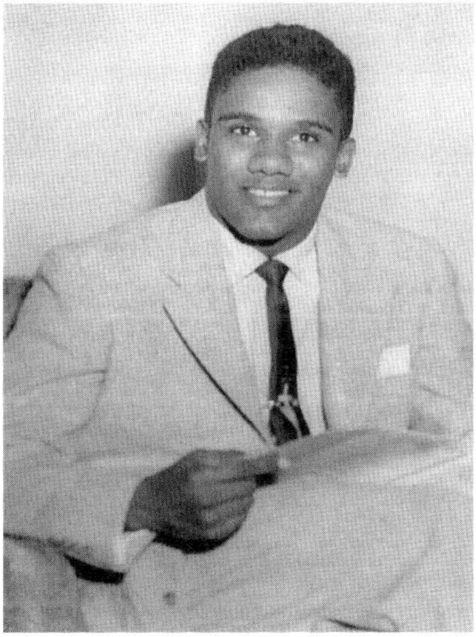

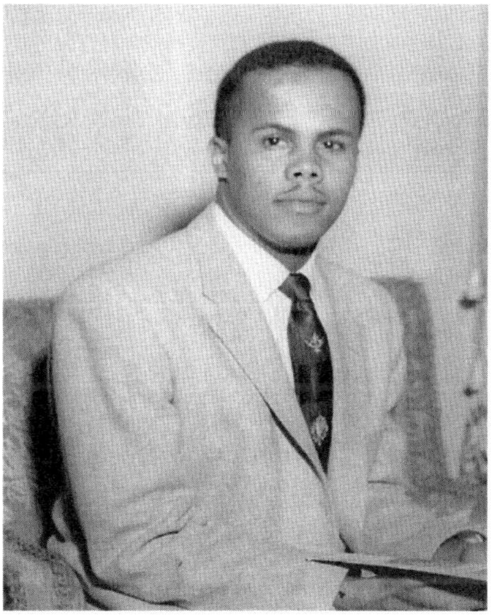

Above, left: Walter Williams.

Above, right: Byron Williams.

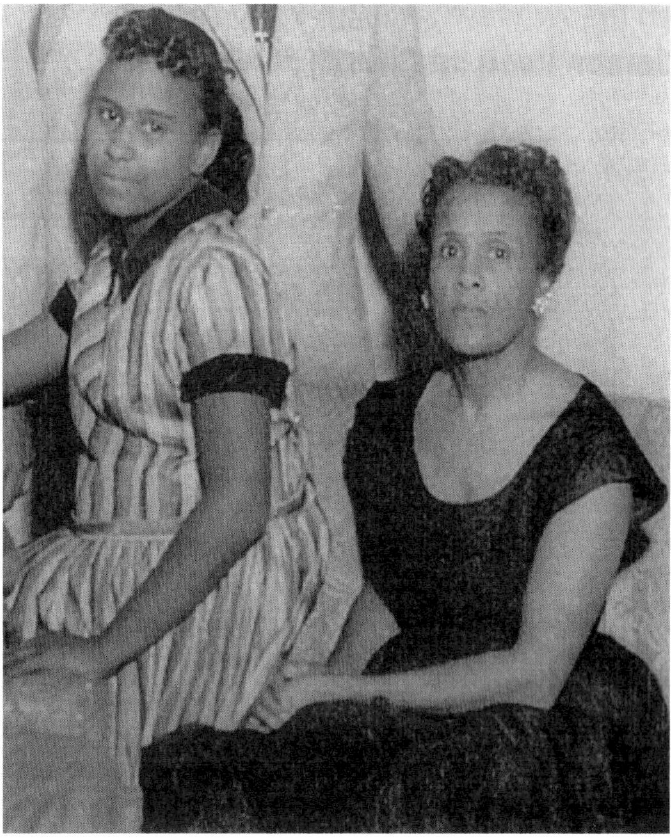
Ruthie Williams, age nine, with her mother, Mrs. Nellie Williams.

Ruth worked in Louisiana after completing her college degree. She then returned to Mississippi for two years to work with the Community Action Agency. She went to graduate school at Howard University in Washington, D.C., where she earned both her master's and doctoral degrees in social work.

Walter "Duke" Williams was a pioneer in civil rights. In November 1943, he was elected president of the Jackson Chamber of Commerce, replacing Dr. C.L. Barnes. In the early 1960s, Duke was elected president of the Urban League's board of directors. The board included twenty African Americans and ten whites. Members C.R. Rutledge was the first vice-president; H. M. Thompson, second vice-president; William D. Lynch, treasurer; Mrs. Carolyn Thomas, secretary; and Harold Goffhelp, assistant secretary. President Williams and his board of directors saved the Urban League from being defunded. Urban League director Fred T. Noland explained the problem as being the lack of local community support for the agency.

Duke's activism in the civil rights movement during the '60s bought him to the attention of the Sovereignty Commission. In later years, when the court ordered the Sovereignty Commission to open its records for inspection to the public, there were documents on Walter Duke Williams. The documents revealed that there had been a "mole" assigned to spy on Williams. In the 1960s throughout the South, sanitation workers, most of whom were African American, began organizing with the help of the NAACP and local civil rights workers. The mole reported to his superiors that Duke Williams was an active supporter of striking sanitation workers. Victor Jones, an official of Security Life Insurance Company, was also watched by a mole from the Sovereignty Commission. The commission files show that the mole reported that Victor Jones was a white male, but in fact, Jones was an extremely light-skinned African American. Interestingly, the mole that spied on Williams was an African American male. While one man was risking his well-being for the rights of his people, he was being deceived by a member of his own race.

The Sovereignty Commission file also contained a pamphlet distributed by striking African American sanitation workers entitled "Why We're on Strike." The pamphlet read as follows:

> *WHY WE'RE ON STRIKE*
>
> *WE'RE ON STRIKE because we must have city recognition of the union we organized to protect our rights.*
>
> *Without a union to establish and protect our rights, we have no way to create better working conditions or make legitimate grievances known. It is a basic American principle that people have a right to organize themselves when they feel that their voice is not being heard.*
>
> *AFSCME (American Federation of the State, County, and Municipal Employees) has signed successful agreements with the city governments in Moss Point and Pascagoula, the two fastest growing cities in the state. Minimum hourly pay for city employees in those cities is now $2.25.*
>
> *WE'RE ON STRIKE because the average wage paid to us (Jackson city garbage workers or other hourly city employees) is one of the lowest in the country. Minimum pay for sanitation workers in Jackson is $3,536. (We take home an average of $50 per week.) In Atlanta, the minimum is $4,548, and in Miami, $5,990.*
>
> *WE'RE ON STRIKE because we have no job security. We can be fired by our immediate supervisor without explanation or notice. There are no hearings or appeal rights. There are no grievance procedures.*

WE'RE ON STRIKE until the City recognizes the union as our representative in collective bargaining. Whether or not the city can meet our demands will be determined in the bargaining talks.

WE WILL RETURN to work when the City Commissioners recognize the union and our representatives with whom to negotiate a contract.

LOCAL No. 1888
AFSCME, AFL-CIO
July 14, 1970

There will be a meeting of the striking city employees at Millsaps College tonight. It will be monitored. Enclosed are samples of the literature being circulated around Jackson.

Duke Williams is the owner of the Penguin Restaurant at the corner of Lynch and Dalton Streets in Jackson. He also owns or has an interest in Security Life Insurance Company. He refuses to allow the restaurant garbage to be picked up. Sanitary conditions around the restaurant are terrible.

Some of the merchants along Farish Street are upset because the city picked up their garbage around 5 a.m. last Sunday Morning. They did not want it picked up.

Warner Buckner is disgusted because he cannot recruit any people to canvas Negro neighborhoods to gather money to assist the strikers. He cannot get any volunteers to assist in voter registration either. He is not prepared to pay for any help; however, it appears he is receiving money from some source. He does not hold a job, but he drives a Volkswagen and states that he has purchased a Pontiac GTO for his wife. He has one child.

Charles Evers is due in Jackson this date, but it is understood he will announce a new chemical plant for Fayette and that he will not get involved in the city employees' strike.

In the late 1950s, Duke organized the men's social club known as the Monday Evening Club. The members were well-known African Americans of Jackson. The club would meet every Monday at the Security Life Insurance building on Lynch Street to discuss the issues involving African Americans in the city. Fifty-one years later, the Monday Evening Club is still in existence. Today, its members include some of Jackson's finest African American men.

The Williams family represented class in its finest form. Even in segregated Jackson, Mississippi, during the early days of Church Street,

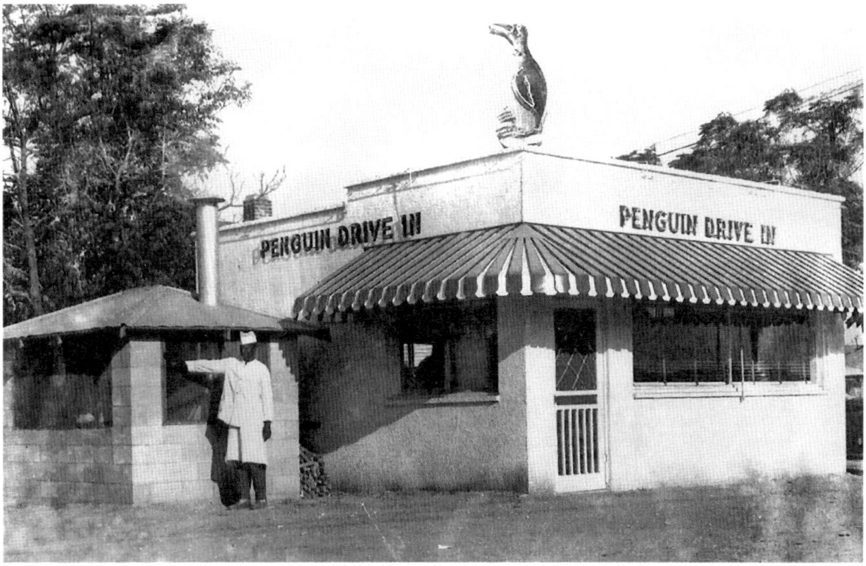

The Penguin Drive-In as it was.

the Williams family lived the American Dream. Ruth Williams is the last survivor of the immediate family, as the males of the family—Duke, Walter and Byron—died first.

Nellie Burbridge Williams lived a long life, having died only a few years ago.

Dr. Ruth Williams recently retired from Jackson State University after completing a long and successful career.

However, the Williams saga continues. In 2011, the following article appeared in the *Clarion-Ledger* newspaper:

> *The Penguin Is Back*
> *By Cassandra Mickens*
>
> *The fabled restaurant and hangout for past Jackson State University students and faculty will return to campus in September on the ground floor of One University Place, said owner and operator John Hardy.*
>
> *Hardy, general manager of the University Club in downtown Jackson for the past 36 years, retired from that post last week to resurrect The Penguin and its beloved hot dog special. "It's two hot dogs piled with coleslaw and french fries and slathered with a spicy barbecue sauce from a special recipe that no one's been able to replicate. It's so different, yet so good," Hardy said.*

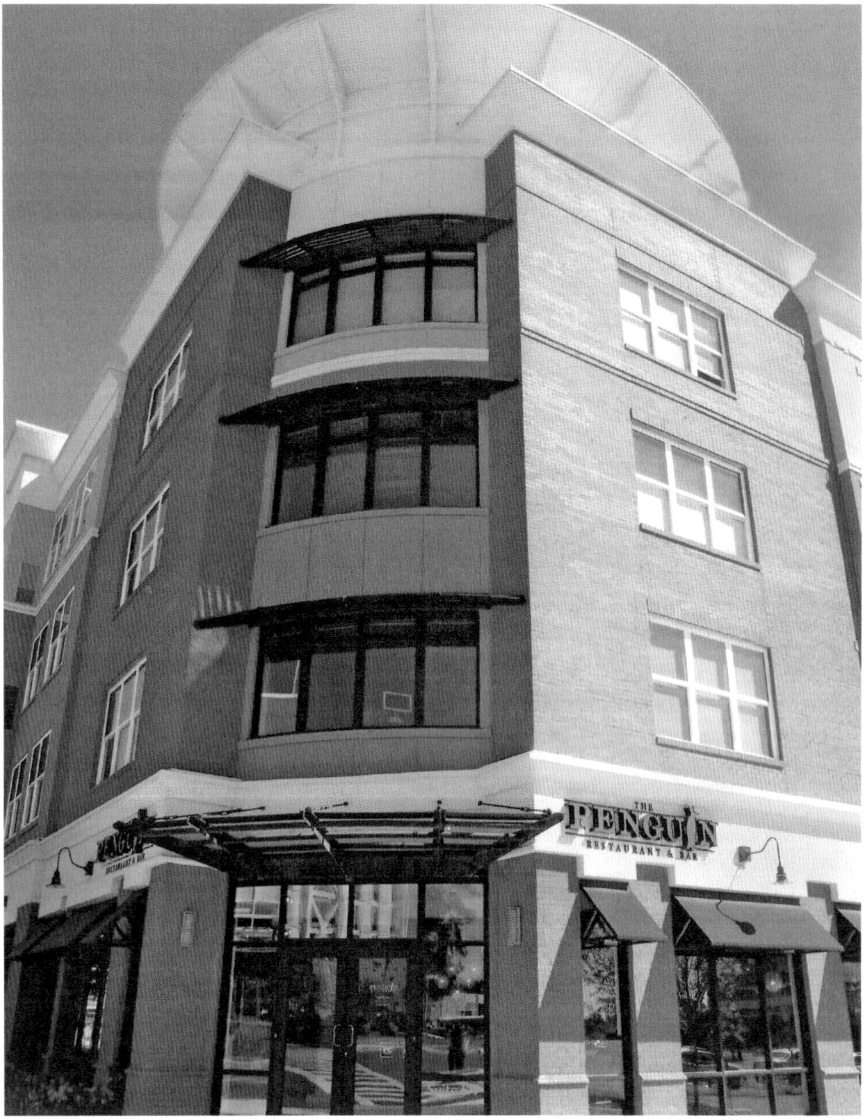

The Penguin Restaurant & Bar, 2011.

Hardy has purchased the recipe from the original owner's family—a guarantee from the new owner that the special will mirror the original.

A group of west Jackson entrepreneurs will open The Penguin, a restaurant at One University Place, in early fall. The original Penguin was located in the same area, and Jackson resident and owner Duke Williams closed the restaurant in the early 1980s. Recently, the City of Jackson awarded the new owners of the Penguin Café two grants.

The new Penguin Restaurant and Bar opened November 9, 2011, and has now become a beacon of light and hope in the west Jackson community. It captures different dining segments with charm and grace, most importantly great food and service. It delivers everything from the Hot Dog Special to Duck ala Orange and everything in between. Hardy wrote the menu taking in consideration the wide customer base the restaurant would have. The Penguin offers southern cuisine with its daily lunch specials that include Red Beans and Rice, Fried Chicken, Beef Brisket, Smothered Pork Chops and Fried Catfish. This is a perfect lunch spot with a $10 daily lunch special that is light on the wallet and heavy in flavor. The Penguin also features a banquet room that seats 80 and is perfect for small receptions up to 124. On the entertainment side, The Penguin features live entertainment on Thursdays, Fridays and Saturdays. To complete the week, The Penguin features a Sunday Brunch from 11:00 a.m. to 3:00 p.m. Other local restaurants would struggle to match its varied menu of Chitterling, Fried Pork Chops, Fried and Baked Chicken, Meatloaf, Turkey and Dressings, Spaghetti and Meat Sauce and Neck Bones and Fried Catfish, just to name a few selections. The Penguin Restaurant & Bar…upscale but not uppity!

Chapter 6

The Lee Family

In the early days, Edward Lee was the patriarch of the Lee family and the kingpin of West Church Street. Lee was born near Hazlehurst, Mississippi, in a community known as Dentville. In later years, Edward Lee Sr. moved to Jackson, Mississippi, where he met his future wife, Allie Hunter. Allie was the daughter of a Mr. Randolph, who owned a successful plumbing company. Mr. Randolph had a beautiful home on the corner of Monument and North Farish Streets and across the street from the future site of the Paris Cleaner. The headquarters of his plumbing business, an army-type Quonset hut, was located at 112 (rear) West Monument Street. Mr. Randolph also owned several rental properties. In other words, he was a "man of means."

After a reasonable courtship and the approval of Mr. Randolph, Edward Lee Sr. married Allie Hunter. This union produced two boys, Eddie Lee and Edward Lee Jr., and the family became faithful members of Central United Methodist Church on North Farish Street. After completing high school, Eddie Lee graduated from Tuskegee, while Edward Lee Jr. graduated from Blue Field State College in West Virginia. Eddie was employed by the United States Veterans Administration and became the first African American loan officer in the district that covered Alabama and Mississippi. Edward Lee Jr. served many years as a counselor at the Boys Reformatory School in Raymond, Mississippi.

Edward Lee Sr. was a very successful businessman. He opened the Edward Lee Hotel in the 100 block of West Church in the early 1930s and later acquired the Mill and Oakley Café. Like his father-in-law, Edward Lee Sr. also owned several rental properties. During the segregated 1940s, '50s and '60s, the two main Jackson hotels open to African Americans were the Edward Lee Hotel and the Summers Hotel. The Summers Hotel, originally the Maples, a rooming house for whites, was located at 619 West Pearl Street. The building was remodeled and renamed Summers Hotel in 1943 after it was purchased by W.J. Summers (1897–1977), a prominent African American businessman.

Mr. Lee was always soft-spoken and impeccably dressed in tailored suits from Oliver's Tailor Shop or the Rogers' Brothers Tailor Shop. Edward Lee was a leader of men and a great organizer. He believed in the young kids of Jackson and contributed to their welfare. He sponsored the Cub and Boy Scouts and contributed to the Bethlehem Center. He also, according to records contained in the Sovereignty Commission files, contributed financially to the civil rights movement of the turbulent days of the early 1960s. Edward Lee Sr. was also the first African American promoter in Mississippi, and his reputation in this field extended beyond the boundaries of Mississippi.

Edward and Allie Lee resided within the Edward Lee Hotel. Edward Lee was the overall manager, and Allie Lee managed the restaurant. In the early days, the hotel boasted one of the finest restaurants in the city of Jackson. Only Shepherd Kitchenette on North Farish Street was considered a better restaurant. The owner of Shepherd Kitchenette, David D. Shepherd, was a well-known chef in the city.

The cooks at the Edward Lee Hotel Restaurant were not without a reputation. Annie Bell, Allie's sister, was well known for her homemade pies, especially the peach cobbler. Muggie Lee "Murk" Bratton Lewis, the second cook in the kitchen, also had a following of faithful customers. In later days, Murk became the cook at the Sun-n-Sand Motel on Lamar Street.

Edward Lee maintained an impressive business office. The walls were covered with pictures of dignitaries who stayed at the hotel. Many notable African American entertainers stayed at the Edward Lee Hotel. It was not uncommon to see buses parked out front on West Church Street with names like The Count Basie Orchestra, Savannah Churchill or B.B. King scribbled on their sides. The big bands of Buddy Johnson, Tiny Bradshaw and Roy Milton were also regular tenants. Once, while barnstorming near Tougaloo College's campus, baseball greats Larry Doby, Jackie Robinson and Satchel Paige stayed at the hotel. Edward Lee also owned two rooming houses in front of the Edward Lee Hotel in which tenants stayed by the week or month.

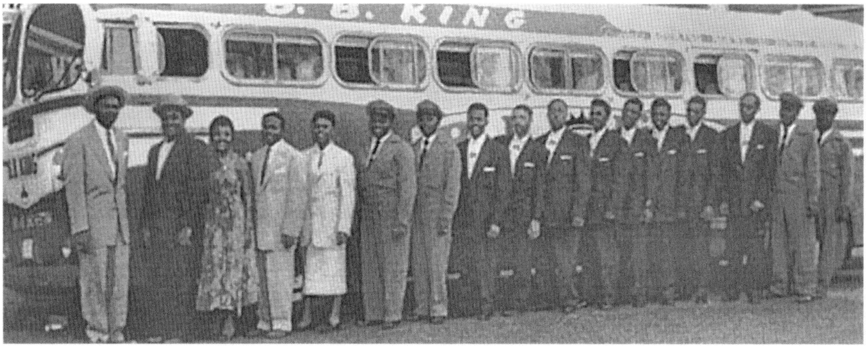

B.B. King and his entourage in front of the Edward Lee Hotel.

As a promoter, Edward Lee booked most of the entertainers who performed at the Stevens Rose Room, the Crystal Palace, the Blue Flame, the Elks Rest and College Park. The second African American promoter in the city during the early days was Willie Miller, who booked entertainers at the Stevens Rose Room and the skating rink that he owned. Miller also owned the *Mississippi Enterprise* newspaper, one of the oldest African American newspapers in the city of Jackson.

In 1941, Edward Lee Sr. secured a contract from the U.S. Army to feed and provide housing for the African American draftees reporting to Hawkins Field. Home Dining Room, owned by prominent African American Mrs. Robinson, had a similar deal with the army. Home Dining Room was located on the corner of Farish Street and Hamilton Street. Unlike Shepherd Kitchenette, Home Dining Room was very conservative, catering mainly to churchgoing folk and gospel quartets.

In addition to having excellent kitchen help, Edward Lee employed a highly qualified office manager, L'Dina Robinson, to help run and manage his vast enterprise. According to Robinson, the Edward Lee Hotel was destroyed by fire in the late 1970s. The mementos, pictures and certificates—all significant pieces of African American history in Jackson—proudly displayed on the wall in his office were all lost.

Edward Lee opened and operated the Mill and Oakley Café in the late 1930s. The café was a wood-frame building located on the corner of Mill and Oakley Streets. Attached to the north side of the building was a shed that covered a huge, open barbeque pit. Mill and Oakley Café was the first African American café to feature an open-pit barbeque and was sometimes used to feed the overflow of African American draftees staying at the hotel. The Mill and Oakley Café was one of the outstanding restaurants during the early days of Church Street. However, there were many other popular cafés in the city in the early 40s: Julius Mitchell operated the Booker T. Grill; Woodrow Biggs operated Club 119, located on North Farish Street; and W.A. Summers, who owned Summers Hotel, owned the Blackstone Café, also on North Farish Street. Other outstanding cafés owned by African Americans included the Blue Light Café, the Harlem Grill, Duck's Café, the Shepherd Kitchenette, Home Dining Room, Eat and Beat It Café and the Doty Grill. In the early 1950s, Edward Lee tore down the Mill and Oakley Café and built a brick building. He rented one side of the building to Luke Palmley, who continued to operate the Mill and Oakley Café until his death. Woodrow Biggs rented the café and continued to operate it until his death. Finally, the Carver Branch Library secured the building and used it for storage. The Mill and Oakley Café was a thriving business for over fifty years.

Edward Lee Sr. participated in many social activities during the early days of Church Street. His favorite by far was his involvement in the L.K. Atwood Elks Lodge. In the late 1930s, Edward Lee, Jack Young, M.E. Mosley, Dr. Smith (Sally Harris Clinic) and W.A. Summers organized the Elks Lodge and named it in honor of African American physician L.K. Atwood. The L.K. Atwood Elks Lodge was originally located on Eric Street just off Bailey Avenue. The group later moved to the Dr. R.O. Williams building on Farish Street before relocating to west Jackson on Lynch Street on several acres of land. It was on this location that a beautiful two-story brick building was constructed, and it was Edward Lee, Jack Young and W.A. Summers who signed the mortgage that covered the cost of this construction. Edward Lee served as the Exalter Rulers of the L.K. Atwood Elks Lodge for many years and booked many famous entertainers to perform at the lodge, which was a very popular spot for African Americans during the 1950s, '60s and '70s.

The Edward Lee Hotel was the first hotel to integrate in Jackson, Mississippi. The story was featured in the *Spokane Chronicle* on Monday, July 20, 1964.

Before the passage of the Civil Rights Act of 1964, there were three other African American hotels in the city of Jackson. In the late 1930s, Fred Scott owned the Hollywood Hotel, which was located on North Farish Street a few doors down from the Farish Street Baptist Church. Then there was the Greystone Hotel on Grayson Street (Lamar Street), which was originally the home of Betty Marino. Bae Buddy converted the elegant home into a hotel around 1950. Betty Marino was a well-known African American teacher, having worked many years at the Smith Robertson School. The first African American YWCA was named in her honor. However, Lee's

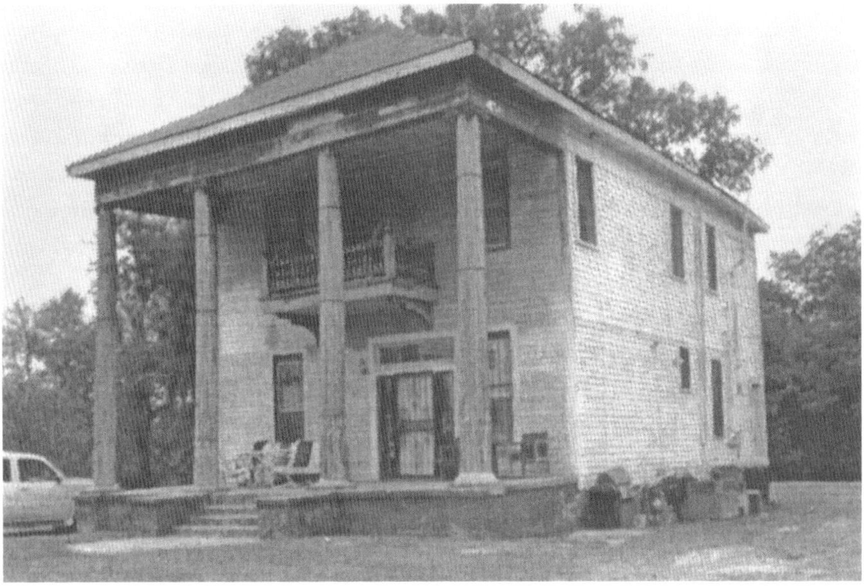

Above: Betty Marino's home became the Greystone Hotel. *Photo by Ben Bradley*.

Below: Bellhops at the King Edward Hotel, 1941.

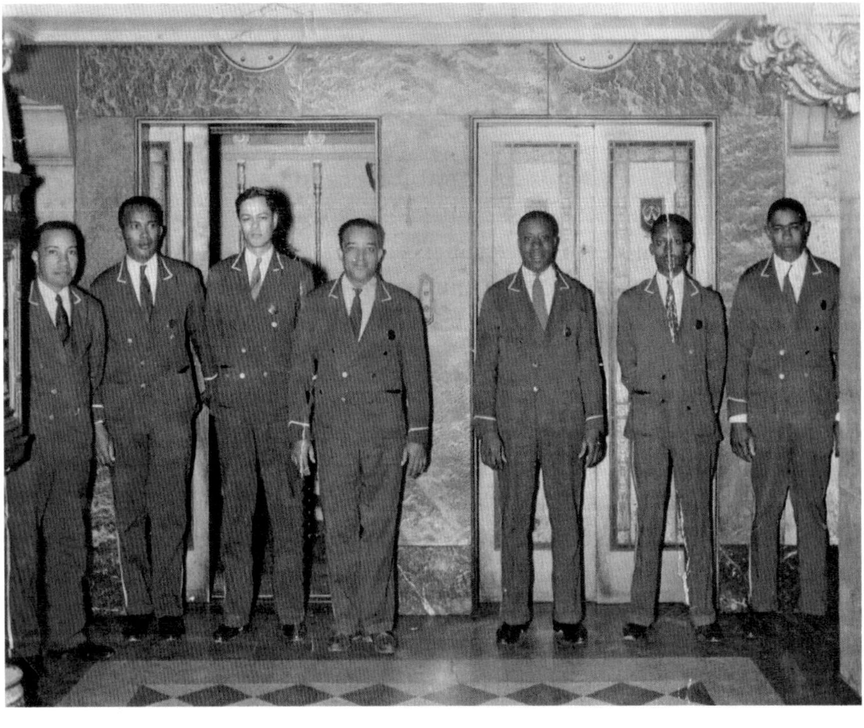

main competitor in the hotel business was W.A. Summers, who established Summers Hotel on East Pearl Street.

In the 1940s, the King Edward Hotel on Capitol Street was the most exclusive facility in the state. It was, however, segregated by race in accordance with Jim Crow laws. Rather than integrate in the late 1960s, the King Edward Hotel closed its doors. It would be nearly fifty years before the King Edward reopened its doors to an integrated public.

Chapter 7
The Hall/Tharp Family

In its early days, Church Street was a popular residential area for several well-to-do African American families, including the Halls and Tharps. Carsie Hall and his wife, Doris Tharp Hall, lived at 131 Church Street, two houses east of the Central United Methodist Parsonage. Doris Tharp Hall was the matriarch of the Tharp family. The Tharp family owned the house next-door to the Halls' house at 129 Church Street. In the early 1960s, the Tharp family also owned several rental houses on George and Bloom Streets, as well as property in Collier Alley. Doris Hall also purchased two houses on Prentiss Street in west Jackson. Carsie Hall was a mail carrier for the United States Post Office. Doris Hall taught school for several years and in the early 1950s became the manager of the College Park Auditorium, located near Jackson State College on Lynch Street.

Doris Tharp Hall was one of five children of Olivia Beatty and J.A. Tharp, a retired bricklayer. Doris's siblings were Sidney, Catherine and a set of twin boys. The twin boys drowned at a school outing at an early age. The three older children attended Holy Ghost Catholic School. Doris Tharp graduated from Tougaloo College in 1929, Sidney Tharp graduated from Howard University in Washington, D.C., and Catherine graduated from Jackson College. Both Doris and Catherine became teachers, while Sidney went on to become a lawyer.

Carsie and Doris Hall had one son, Carsie Hall Jr. Carsie Jr.'s schooling was interrupted in June 1956 when he was arrested for the rape of an African American girl but sentenced only for assault. In 1957, Carsie Hall

Jr. was again tried and convicted of rape. This time he was sentenced to ten years, but through his mother's efforts, he was released early. Upon his release, Carsie Jr. moved to the Mississippi Gulf Coast, where he worked at Ingalls Shipbuilding. He became a supervisor, married and started a family. Carsie Jr. returned to Jackson and lived in the Tharp family home at 129 Church Street. He raised a family of two girls and lived an uneventful life until his death.

In many circles, it is believed that Carsie Jr.'s troubles were brought on by the state of Mississippi in retaliation for Carsie Hall Sr.'s affiliation with the NAACP. In 1955, Carsie Hall Sr. was elected president of the Jackson chapter of the NAACP, the position Dr. A.H. McCoy had held for three years.

Carsie's brother-in-law, Sidney Tharp (who later became the first African American from Jackson to graduate from a law school), encouraged and later convinced him to become a lawyer. The son of Dr. Sidney D. Redmond agreed to tutor Carsie, and he passed the Mississippi Bar in the late 1950s.

DORIS THARP HALL

Doris Tharp Hall was a successful realtor and a devoted community worker. She was a strong supporter of her alma mater, Tougaloo College, having graduated in 1929. In fact, the first meeting held to organize the Jackson Tougaloo Alumni Club was held in Doris's home. Doris served as the president of the Alpha Kappa Alpha Sorority, Inc. and often enjoyed hosting its meetings in her home. She also entertained the Ivy Leaf members with tasty food as they made plans for activities such as Negro History Week. Doris gave back to the community and became one of the most popular and successful people in Jackson. She was known to open savings accounts for needy kids in the community, and she also developed a parcel of land behind the house on Church Street into a softball field for kids within the community. Doris once served as treasurer for the NAACP's Mississippi chapter and was affiliated with the Heroines of Jericho in the 1950s.

Doris Hall became the manager of the College Park Auditorium in the 1950s. This was a prestigious position for Dorothy, but it also caused her some problems, as she soon became a target of the Mississippi State Sovereignty Commission. There was a note contained in the files of the commission that read in part, "Carsie Hall's wife, Doris Hall, is the manager of the College

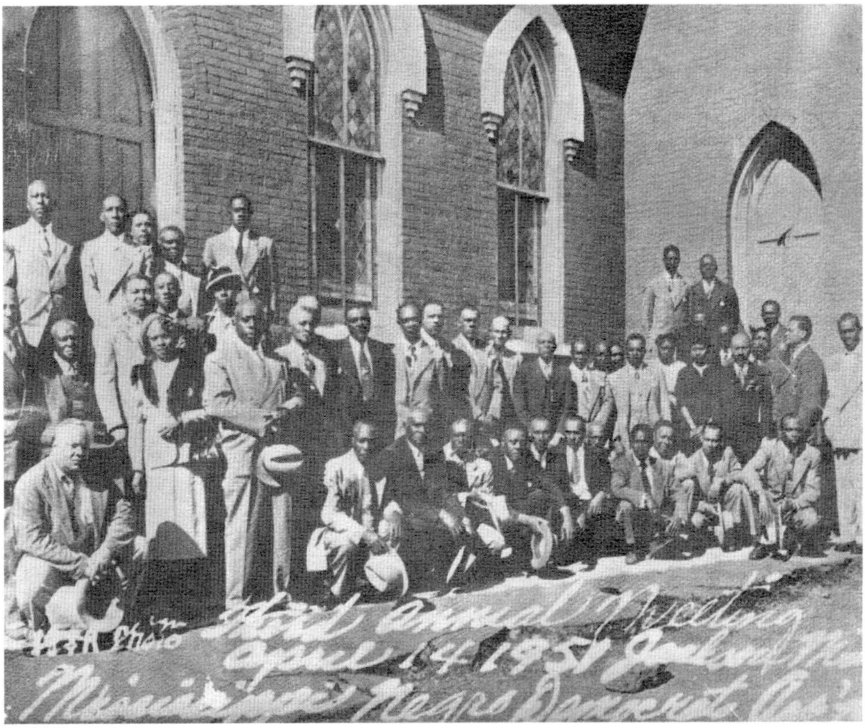

First annual meeting of the Mississippi Negro Democrat Association, April 14, 1951.

Park Auditorium on Lynch Street in Jackson. Due to her employment, it is believed that Doris will temper Carsie Hall's activities should they endanger her security." At the same time, her position with the state gave her some leverage in negotiating a lesser sentence for Carsie Jr., who had been given ten years for rape.

Like her husband, Doris Hall was also spied upon by the Mississippi Sovereignty Commission. The following entry was found in her Sovereignty Commission files:

> *Regarding the two homes in a previously all-white neighborhood on South Prentiss Street being purchased by Negroes, the following was learned: Doris Hall, colored female, is the wife of Negro attorney Carsie Hall. She supervises the College Park Auditorium. She and her husband are active in Civil Rights activities. She purchased the two homes—one of them from the Federal Housing Administration (FHA), and the other from a private owner. These residences were bought to rent out. Doris Hall has mentioned*

that she may rent one of them to a group of white girls associated with the Mount Beulah group. She is still debating whether or not she should do this. She is Alvin Bronstein's landlady.

Sadly, the investigator making this report to the Sovereignty Commission was an African American. Alvin Bronstein was mentioned in the report due to the fact that he was a Jew and also the head of the first Legal Service Unit, located in Dr. R.O. Williams's building at 603 North Farish Street in Jackson.

Following is Mrs. Doris Hall's obituary. She was laid to rest in the Greenwood Cemetery:

Mrs. Doris Tharp Hall was the second child of the late Junious and Olivia Tharp of Jackson, Mississippi. She was christened as a baby at Holy Ghost Catholic Church in Jackson, Mississippi.

Mrs. Hall attended elementary and high school at Holy Ghost Catholic School. She graduated with a B.A. degree from Tougaloo College.

She was a dedicated teacher for many years. She retired as Director of Recreation for the City of Jackson. She was a member of the Ladies Auxiliary at Holy Ghost Church. Mrs. Hall was also active with many organizations, including the Mary Church Terrell Literary Arts Club, the Mississippi State Federation of Colored Women's Club and the Smith Robertson Museum and Cultural Center. Mrs. Hall was an outstanding community leader.

Mrs. Hall was joined in holy matrimony with attorney Carsie A. Hall, and to this union was born a son, Carsie Alvin Hall Jr.

She departed this life Friday, May 20, 1988.

Mrs. Hall leaves to cherish many memories: her husband; son, Carsie Alvin Hall Jr., grandchildren, Earline (Robert) Shearry, Evelyn (Quentin) McKay, Catherine O. Hall, Carsie Alvin Hall III and Doris M. Hall; one sister-in-law, Christine M. Tharp; one niece, Lisa T. Bell; one nephew, Sidney Tharp Jr.; and a host of other relatives and friends.

CARSIE A. HALL, ATTORNEY AT LAW

Carsie Hall was truly a gentleman and was highly respected among his peers. Even a spy with the Sovereignty Commission reported the following: "Hall is a person who likes publicity, but at the same time, he is not believed

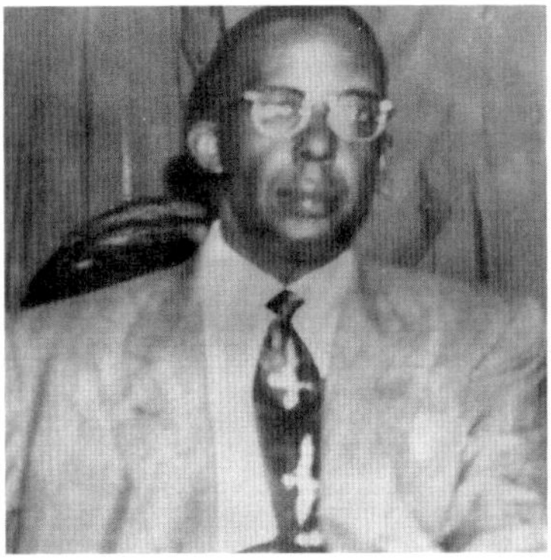

Left: Attorney Carsie Hall lived on Church Street and was also a postman.

Below: *From left to right*: Honorable Jack Young, Marian Wright Edelman, Honorable R. Jess Brown and Honorable Carsie H. Hall Sr. discuss the NAACP defense fund. These African-American men are now part of history, as two mail carriers and a shop teacher who wanted to become lawyers in segregated Mississippi changed America forever. Their journey was not easy, but the work of these three men in the 1950s and '60s set the stage for the Freedom Riders, the Civil Rights Workers and Title VII of the Civil Rights Act of 1964.

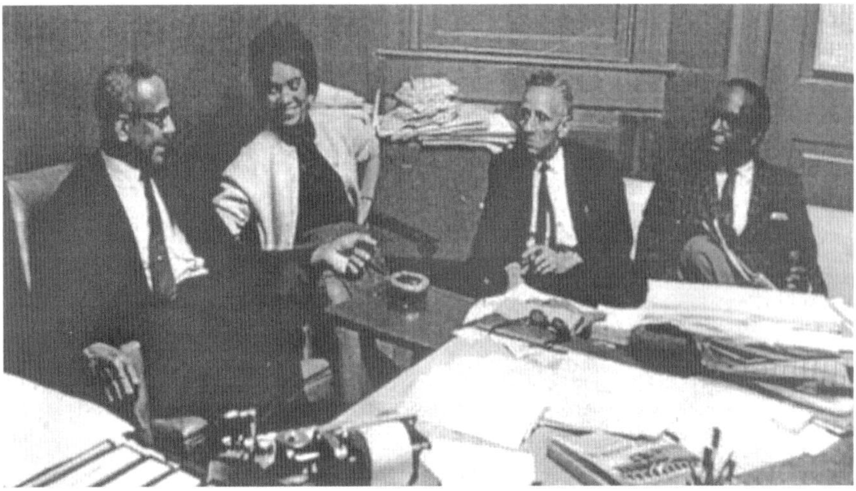

to be a person who would advocate and carry out mass demonstrations and picketing. Likewise, he is not believed to be the type to resort to violence or the promotion of violence." Carsie Hall played a major role in the early stages of the civil rights movement in Jackson.

Carsie A. Hall was elected president of the Jackson chapter of the NAACP. He was opposed by Reverend Allen Johnson of Pratt Memorial Methodist Church, located on Pascagoula Street. Hall supported the formation of the Mississippi Freedom Democratic Party and was elected a delegate to the county convention. He was one of the founders of the Magnolia Bar Association along with attorneys James A. Barnes, Meridian; Mayor Benjamin Green, Mound Bayou; Emette Perkins, Natchez; Onette Johnson, Prentiss; Jack H. Young Sr., Jackson; and R. Jess Brown, Vicksburg. These eight lawyers constituted practically the entire black bar of Mississippi. James A. Barnes was elected the first president of the Magnolia Bar and

THE EARLY BLACK POSTMEN

Notable families come and go. They make these contributions to society and return to their maker. But their legacy lives on through their contributions to community, church, politics and family life. Such were the contributions of the early black postmen, who had to be a cut above the rest in order to become professionals in an occupation that had been closed to the black race.

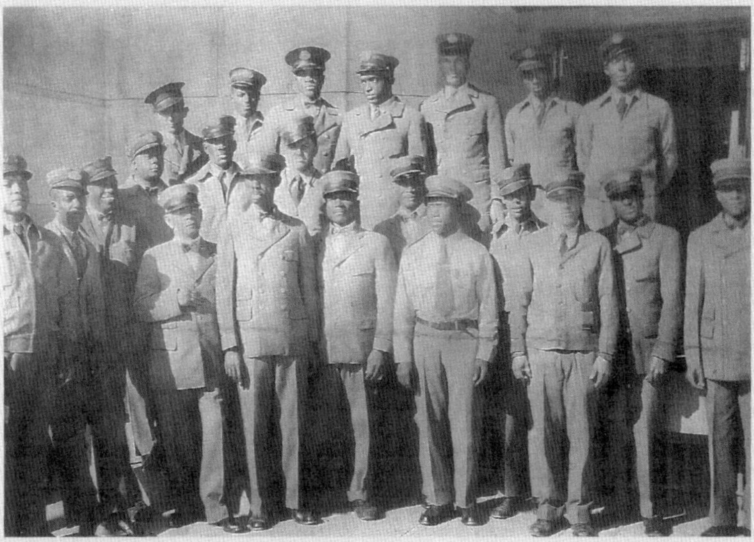

The African American postmen.

served until his death in the late 1950s. He was succeeded by Sidney R. Tharp, who served until the late 1960s.

The Council of Federated Organizations (COFO) was formed in Mississippi in 1962. Reverend R.L.T. Smith, the owner of Smith's Grocery Store, on Valley Street, was named treasurer. Attorney Carsie Hall was chosen as secretary, and Bob Moses was appointed the statewide project director.

Carsie Hall's law office was first located in the 100 block of North Farish Street in a building owned by Dr. A.H. McCoy. He later moved his office to the Crystal Palace building, owned by Georgia Hodge, in the 500 block of North Farish Street. Carsie often reflected on his journey to become a lawyer with others. He once told a friend, "As a letter carrier, I delivered the mail at the Heidelberg…in Jackson. I entered the building through the front door and rode the main elevator. But when I came to the Heidelberg to take the bar exam, I had to enter through the rear door and ride the freight elevator."

Carsie Hall served as the second chair with famed attorney William M. Kunstler of New York City. In his final days, Carsie was the director of a legal service funded by the Office of Economics Opportunity (OEO). Carsie Hall Sr.; his wife, Doris Hall; and son, Carsie Jr. all died within a two-year period of each other. Carsie Hall is more famous in death than when he walked the streets of Jackson.

SIDNEY R. THARP, ATTORNEY AT LAW

Attorney Sidney Tharp was attorney Hall's brother-in-law, and he once lived next door to him at 129 Church Street. Sidney was married to Christine M. Tharp, who was a counselor and math teacher in the Jackson Public School System. Sidney and Christine were an attractive couple. Unlike Carsie Hall, Sidney was flamboyant and outspoken, and he had been a lawyer all of his adult life.

Sidney Tharp did not accept civil rights cases. However, there is one instance in which he was allegedly hired by the family of Professor Clemmon King. When Professor King attempted to integrate Southern University, the State of Mississippi had him placed in an insane asylum. When attorney Tharp sought a court order to release Clemmon King, the judge instead ejected Tharp from the legal proceedings with the allegation that he was under the influence of alcohol or "goof balls." Attorney R. Jess Brown, a civil rights attorney, became the attorney of record for Clemmon King.

Tharp's office was located at 406 North Farish Street in the building that was owned by Sidney R. Redmond and housed in the Big Apple Inn. Attorney Tharp had a lucrative law practice, handling all types of cases—except civil rights cases. One particular case handled by Tharp involved Reverend Curtis West's complaint against the Greater Clark Street Baptist Church. Reverend West was promptly reinstated as pastor. Attorney Tharp also had a monopoly on DUI cases and other misdemeanor cases involving African Americans. The Mississippi Sovereignty Commission described attorney Sidney R. Tharp as being one of Jackson's "foremost Negro citizens."

Attorney Sidney R. Tharp was a great orator, a consummate lawyer and one of the best-dressed professional persons who frequented the Farish Street district in the early days of Church Street. He died years before Carsie, so his reputation as a lawyer is not as well remembered as his brother-in-law's.

Chapter 8
The Conic Family

The patriarch of the Conic family was John Edgar Conic Sr. He was born in 1882 and lived at 218 Church Street with his wife and family. Mr. Conic departed from this earth at the early age of sixty-six, but he left a legacy that included strong family ties, entrepreneurship, love of his church and a strong determination to succeed. The Conic family played a major role in the development of the historic Farish Street business district.

Around Christmas in 1948, the body of John Edgar Conic was found late on a Sunday in a lake behind a lumberyard located in west Jackson. The body was discovered several days after his death by John Dow, an African American who lived on Lynch Street. Mr. Conic's body was riddled with five bullets fired from a .22 caliber pistol. His family had reported to the authorities that he was missing on December 9, 1948. It was determined that the motive was robbery and car theft. Mr. Conic's automobile surfaced in Chicago, Illinois, soon after the murder, and this became the first lead in the murder case. Mount Helm Baptist Church raised $500 to be posted as a reward for the capture of the individual or individuals guilty of this crime. The *Chicago Defender* also offered a $500 reward.

Mr. Conic's funeral was held on Tuesday, December 21, 1948, at his beloved mother church, First Temple, on the corner of Monument and Lamar Streets. A chairman of the deacons, Mr. Conic began his service at Christ Temple Church in 1905. He was a dedicated and dutiful convention member to the district, diocese and national conventions.

At the time of his death, he was actively serving as the chairman of the trustee board and district missionary of Sunday school and Holiness Young People's Union. Mr. Conic was buried in the Elmwood Cemetery in the Georgetown area of Jackson.

Eventually, a young eighteen-year-old African American named James Vials Nicholas was captured and convicted for the murder of Mr. John Edgar Conic Sr. Nicholas testified that after he shot Conic, he drove to the brickyard pond and took money and a watch from the dead man's pockets before dumping the body in the water. Nicholas said he then picked up a fifteen-year-old girl, Martha Jackson, drove to Chicago and lived with her there until he was arrested by the FBI and returned to Jackson. He was sentenced to twenty-five years in the Mississippi State Penitentiary but was freed some twenty years later in 1974. There is no record of who collected the rewards posted by Mount Helm Baptist Church and the *Chicago Defender* newspaper.

After Bishop Jones split from Mount Helm Baptist Church, the Conic family played a major role in the success of his development of the Church of Christ (Holiness) U.S.A. John Edgar Conic's brother, Bishop J.L.I. Conic, served as bishop of the northern diocese from 1927 to 1939.

Bishop J.L.I. Conic was born in Lexington, Mississippi, on October 15, 1876. He established a church in Arkansas and two churches in Mississippi. He also served as pastor of Christ Temple in Jackson and president of CMI College. Bishop J.L.I. Conic was the father of three children: James, Alma and Major Rudd, who also became a Bishop. Bishop Conic died in 1939 in Jackson.

John Edgar Conic's nephew, Bishop Major Rudd Conic, was born on December 22, 1909. Bishop Major Conic spent time in Jackson, Arkansas and Alabama. At eight years old, he attended CMI College. He graduated from Dunbar High School in Washington, D.C. In 1928, he returned to Jackson as a teacher at the CMI College for two years and later became the school's president, serving in that position for four years. In 1953, the National Executive Council appointed Bishop Major Conic as pastor of the Christ Temple Church in Chicago, Illinois, and presiding bishop of the northern and western dioceses.

The Business Ventures of Mr. John Edgar Conic

John Edgar Conic Sr. was the father of three boys—John Edgar Conic Jr., Lemuel Conic and Frank N. Conic—and two daughters, Falba Ruth Conic and Myrtle Conic.

John Edgar Conic Sr. operated the City Barber Shop, located in the 100 block of North Farish Street. This barbershop was located in the same block as the offices of Dr. Sidney Redmond, Dr. A.H. McCoy and attorney W.L. Mhoon. The City Barber Shop was the largest African American barbershop in the city of Jackson. It was at the City Barber Shop where Conic trained all of his boys to be barbers. John Edgar Conic Jr. and Frank N. Conic became successful barbers and eventually owned their own barbershops. Conic Sr. eventually sold the City Barber Shop to Mr. Foster, a tailor who had previously rented space from Mr. Conic for his shop.

For thirty years, John Edgar Conic Sr. was the only independent contractor with the *Chicago Defender* and the *Pittsburg Courier* newspapers in the city of Jackson, circulating these papers throughout the city. By the start of World War I, the *Chicago Defender* was the nation's most influential black weekly newspaper, with more than two thirds of its readership base located outside of Chicago. During the war, the paper utilized its influence to wage a successful campaign in support of the Great Migration. It published blazing editorials, articles and cartoons lauding the benefits of the North, posted job listings and train schedules to facilitate relocation and declared May 15, 1917, as the date of the "Great Northern Drive." The *Chicago Defender*'s support of the Great Migration caused southern readers to migrate to the North in record numbers. Between 1916 and 1918, at least 110,000 African Americans migrated to Chicago, nearly tripling the city's black population.

The *Pittsburgh Courier* was once the country's most widely circulated black newspaper, with a national circulation of almost 200,000. Established in 1907 by Edwin Harleston, a security guard and aspiring writer, the newspaper gained national prominence after attorney Robert Lee Vann took over as editor-publisher, treasurer and legal counsel in 1910. By the 1930s, it was one of the top-selling black newspapers in the country—as widely read as the *Chicago Defender* and the *Afro-American*.

From the beginning, the *Courier* called for improvements in housing, health and education and protested the slum conditions in which black people were forced to live in Pittsburgh and elsewhere throughout the nation. In one campaign, it pressed for an increase of black physicians in the Pittsburgh area and the opening of an African American hospital to serve the community's health needs, as white facilities were unwilling to treat African Americans.

At the time of his death, John Edgar Conic Sr. was still an independent contractor with the *Chicago Defender* and the *Pittsburg Courier* newspapers. It was the aforementioned eighteen-year-old African American male with a Saturday night special who terminated the contracts in December 1949.

Penny News Stand, located in the 100 block of North Farish Street, started handling the sale of the *Pittsburg Courier* and *Chicago Defender* newspapers after Conic Sr.'s death. Mr. Armstrong, the owner of Penny News Stand, was also a photographer.

FRANK N. CONIC

Amid tragedy, the Conic family still flourished. Frank N. Conic owned Superior Barber Shop before his father was killed. However, in the early part of 1950, the ownership of Superior Barber Shop passed to John Edgar Conic Jr. because Frank and Doris Conic established the Conic Beauty and

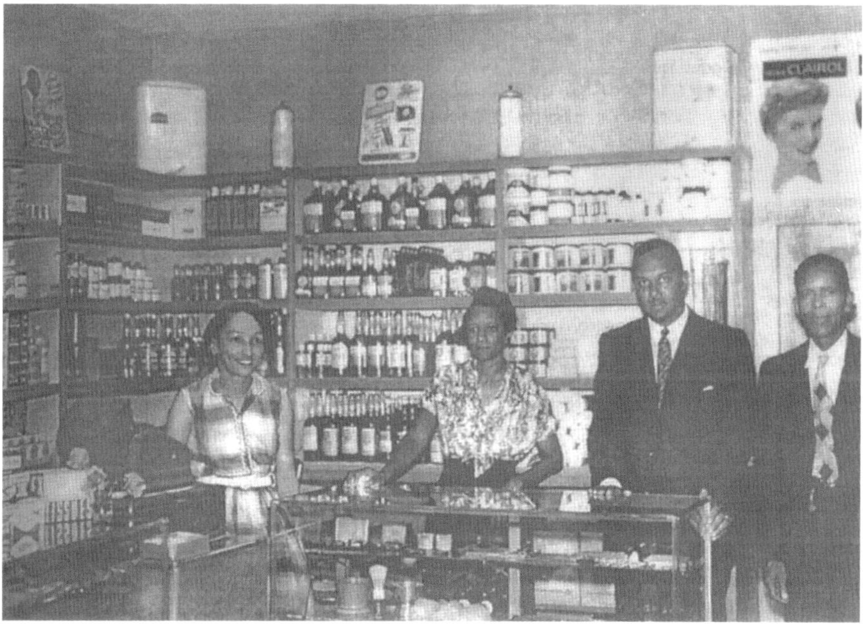

Conic Beauty and Barber Supply operated from 1950 to 1975 at 615 North Farish Street. *From left to right*: Doris V. Conic, Myrtle C. Johnson, Frank N. Conic and Jack Johnson.

Barber Supply at 615 North Farish Street. Conic Beauty Supply was the first company to bring to Mississippi perm hair straighteners for African American women. Frank N. Conic successfully operated the Conic Beauty and Barber Supply for twenty-five years, retiring in 1975.

Frank N. Conic lived on the hill at 240 East Church Street. His sister, Mrs. Myrtle C. Johnson, also lived on Church Street in the family home and worked for her brother at Conic Beauty and Barber Supply. Myrtle's husband, Jack Johnson, had a business within Conic Beauty and Barber Supply known as Johnson Lock and Key.

Before Frank N. Conic retired, his company was delivering beauty supplies all over the state of Mississippi, and his sales had grossed more than any other African American business in the city of Jackson. Notwithstanding the many successes of this family, there were also a number of tragedies:

—John Edgar Conic Jr.'s wife was killed in a fire at their home on Lynch Street.
—Lemuel Conic, a brother, was severely crippled in one leg.
—Falba Ruth Conic, sister, was confined to a wheelchair.
—Myrtle C. Johnson's son accidentally killed a childhood friend.
—John Edgar Conic Sr. was robbed and murdered.

HAPPIER TIMES

The following is a letter written by Frank N. Conic to Mayor Allen Thompson on June 10, 1960:

240 E. Church St.
Jackson, Miss.
June 10, 1960
The Honorable Allen Thompson
Mayor of Jackson, Miss.

Dear Mr. Mayor,

As a lifelong resident of Jackson, I am proud of the progress that the city has made under your capable leadership. When I ride over this city, it is indeed thrilling for me to realize that my taxes have contributed to its expansion, improvements and beautification.

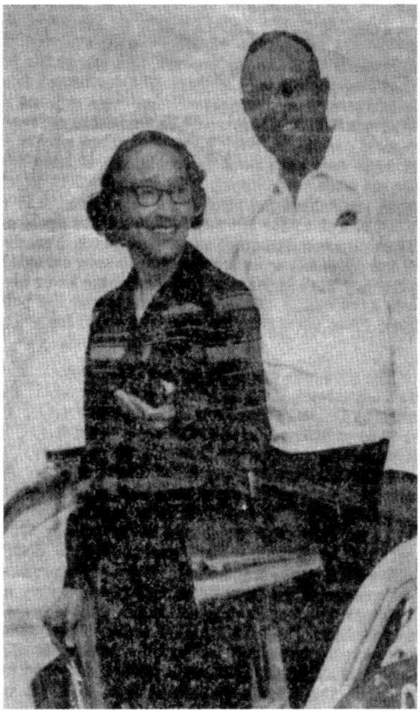

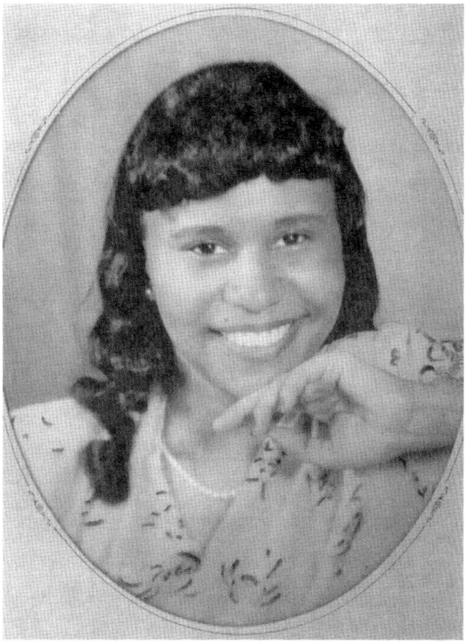

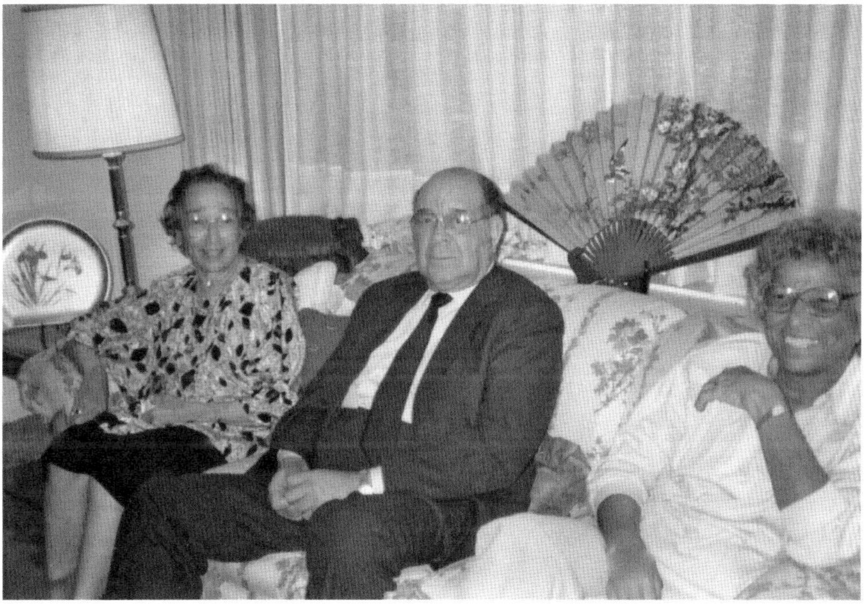

Top, left: Myrtle and Frank Conic.

Top, right: Falba Ruth Conic was a typist for the *Clarion-Ledger*.

Bottom: Doris Conic with her brother and his wife.

Though my portion of the taxes would be minute if it were separated from the total, so would that paid by its wealthiest citizens. Therefore, all of the facilities and projects that the city provides should be available to all of its people, and they should rejoice whenever any proposals are made to improve this community economically and culturally.

So, as one who has confidence in the future of Jackson, I shall vote for the bond issue on next Tuesday. Nevertheless, my enthusiasm is weakened somewhat by the fear that not all Jacksonians will be able to enjoy the benefits that its passage would provide.

You see, sir, I am a Negro, and along with the other members of my race, I am barred from the existing "white" recreational and cultural facilities. The lone exception, I understand, is the municipal auditorium, where colored people may see the wrestling matches.

Evidently, persons who grant us this "privilege" do not believe that Negroes' tastes for culture and entertainment are as varied as those of the white citizens. To assume that colored people are interested only in wrestling is as ridiculous as the assumption that white women [illegible], *so no consideration has been shown to the ladies of my race.*

In making this criticism, I am speaking only for myself, but the sentiments I express are identical to those felt by all of Jackson's worthy Negroes—the kind that you have praised several times.

I want you to know, Mr. Mayor, that I think the citizens are fortunate to have a man of your stature at the head of the city. With your leadership, I am certain that Jackson's progress will increase abundantly in every way during the remainder of your administration.

Sincerely yours,

Frank N. Conic.

Although a portion of the letter is illegible, I believe the intended words were along the lines of "that white women were the only ones to enjoy the finer things in life…." Another point of interest is the fact that the letter was typed by Falba Ruth Conic, Frank's sister and a typist employed by the *Clarion-Ledger*. This letter was featured in the "African American News" section of the *Ledger* and later appeared in the files of the Mississippi State Sovereignty Commission.

After the death of her father, Falba, a wheelchair-bound invalid born in 1916 on Church Street, kept the Conic legacy alive by writing social news

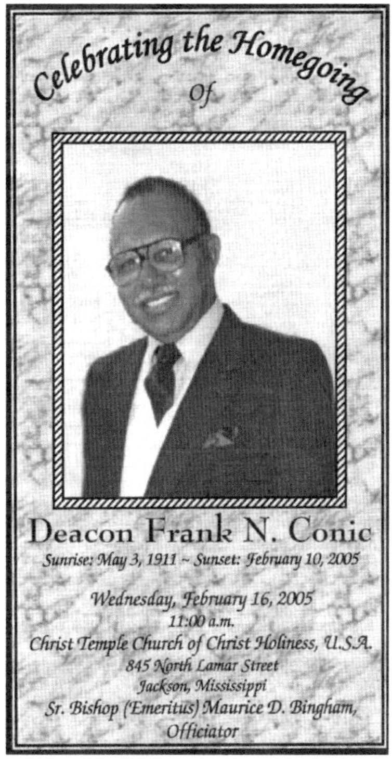
Celebrating the Homegoing
Of
Deacon Frank N. Conic
Sunrise: May 3, 1911 ~ Sunset: February 10, 2005
Wednesday, February 16, 2005
11:00 a.m.
Christ Temple Church of Christ Holiness, U.S.A.
845 North Lamar Street
Jackson, Mississippi
Sr. Bishop (Emeritus) Maurice D. Bingham,
Officiator

articles for the *Chicago Defender*. During this time after thousands of blacks had migrated to Chicago, it would appear that those left behind in Mississippi and those in Chicago yearned for the news and connections of family and community. The *Chicago Defender* newspaper provided that information in its social columns. Falba, through her weekly social articles, made sure that the readers were aware of the parties, birthdays, school trips, vacations, funerals and other community events in Jackson. For example, Falba reported in 1948 that Mrs. George A. Thomas of Cohea Street visited her sister Frances Reed in Chicago and Mr. and Mrs. Joseph Roots of Ludlow Street visited their daughters in Detroit.

The Conics' eldest daughter, Myrtle Conic Buckley Johnson, lived in the

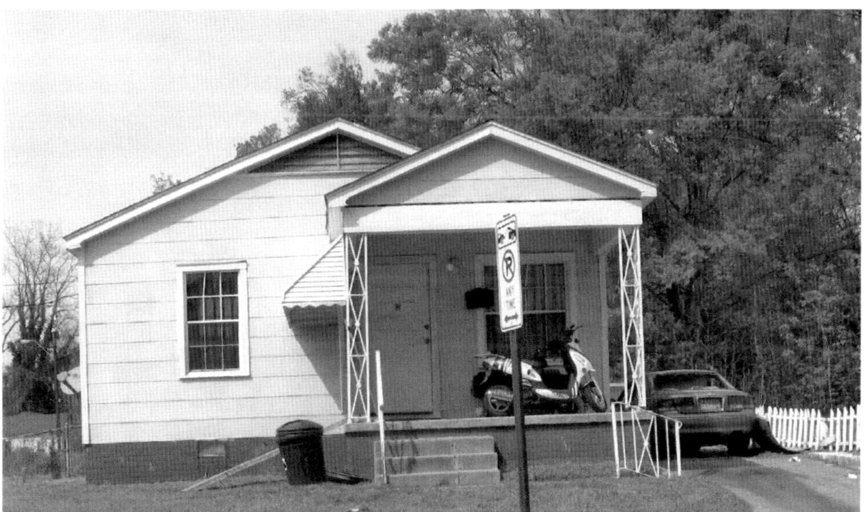

Top: Frank Conic.

Bottom: Myrtle Conic's home. *Photo by Ben Bradley*.

family house on Church Street with her son, Billy Buckley, and second husband, Mr. Johnson. Myrtle worked many years for her brother at Conic Beauty Supply and for her husband, who owned Johnson Lock and Key. Myrtle Johnson was identified as the lady who drove the black falcon automobile.

Frank and Myrtle were the last of the Conic children to pass away. At one time, they were cared for in the same nursing home (Compere's Nursing Home). They lived long lives.

Myrtle Johnson seldom missed a day away from the job. She remained on East Church all of her life, some eighty-plus years. The black falcon automobile was never sold and remained in the garage in the back of her home for many years. Myrtle was truly a person of Church Street.

Frank N. Conic died on February 16, 2005, joining his wife, who had died earlier. The legacy of the Conic family remains in the hearts of those who remember the earlier days of Church Street.

Chapter 9

The Shinault Family

John W. Shinault was truly an unsung hero among the residents of Church Street during the early days. Shinault lived in the last house on East Church Street, in front of Dr. R.O. Williams's home. The Shinault home was located at the corner of Church Street and Grayson Street (later changed to Lamar Street), just a stone's throw from the historic Greenwood Cemetery. John Shinault was married and the father of two beautiful daughters: Charlotte and Johnetta.

John Shinault served as the principal of the Mississippi School for the Negro Deaf in the late 1930s and the early 1940s. Although Shinault received a modest salary, he served for many years as the school's principal.

The Mississippi School for the Negro Deaf was established in 1854. From the earliest detection of a hearing problem, the school provided children with the communication skills and confidence they would need to live happy, productive lives. Plagued by a shortage of teachers in its early years, the school would often close. The school also closed during the Civil War, when the Confederate army used the building as a hospital. In 1857, however, Lawrence Saunders, the school's first student, returned as a full-time teacher. The school never again had to close for lack of instructors, as Saunders continued to teach there until he was killed in an accident on Christmas Day 1895.

The white and black schools for the deaf were integrated in 1965, but even after the racial barrier had been broken down, deaf African Americans still had to face the identity question of whether they were

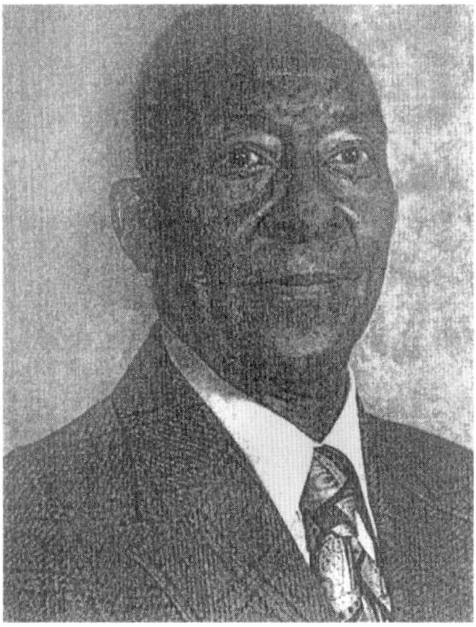

John Shinault, principal of the Mississippi School for the Negro Deaf.

black first or deaf first. John W. Shinault was hired into this atmosphere, and in time, he elevated the status of the Mississippi School for the Negro Deaf to another level. Shinault developed an outstanding athletic program at his school, including an especially impressive basketball team. The team's coach, Eugene Dorsey, is a member of the Dorsey family of Tougaloo, Mississippi, which at one point operated a motel and a jukebox business in Tougaloo. Eugene was a successful coach during his tenure at the Mississippi School for the Negro Deaf. In 1965, the word "Negro" was removed from the school's name.

On April 10, 1985, the board of trustees of the Mississippi School for the Deaf and the Mississippi School for the Blind dedicated Cottage A on the campus in honor of John W. Shinault for his years of service to the Mississippi School for the Deaf. Cottage A is one of three elementary dormitories built in the 1980s. When constructed, the primary purpose of the cottage was to house female students aged five to twelve. As originally designed, the building presently serves as a residence for young girls.

The guests for the dedication of Cottage A included the Honorable Robert Clark, state representative; Dr. R.E. Willis, pastor of College Hill Baptist Church; and Dr. Alma Alexander, superintendent of the Mississippi School for the Deaf. This occasion was the culmination of a great man's career. Shinault was a man with a deep understanding of the culture of children with hearing impairments.

John W. Shinault had previously received the Boy Scouts of America's Certificate of Appreciation Award on January 19, 1973. The certificate cited Shinault as being loyal and an outstanding supporter of the Boy Scouts.

John W. Shinault, the unsung hero, touched the lives of many deaf African Americans. Like so many of the residents of Church Street in the early days, he made major contributions toward providing a better life for the less fortunate.

Chapter 10

Dr. R.O. Williams Family

Dr. Rudolph O. Williams was born in Georgia on August 8, 1912, the son of Blanche and Ida Fennigan Williams. Williams graduated from Meharry Medical College and later served a tour in the U.S. Army, achieving the rank of major. He married Miss Peggy Burnett of Terry, Mississippi.

Dr. Williams lived at 339 Church Street for many years with his wife, Peggy. They were members of Mount Helm Baptist Church, which was located at 301 East Church Street. Dr. Williams's house was built on the lot where Mount Helm constructed its first church in 1868. His beautiful home is still standing and owned by Patricia White. John W. Shinault lived in the house directly in front of Dr. Williams, and just a few doors down was the home of Evangeline Byrd.

Dr. Williams started his medical practice on the second floor of the Paris Cleaners building in the mid-1940s. The Paris Cleaners building, a newly constructed building located on the corner of North Farish and East Monument Streets, was owned by Jessie Williams, an African American. Williams purchased a new fleet of delivery vans, and Paris Cleaners soon became a thriving business and employed a dozen people. Each van driver had a specific route for picking up and delivering clothes to and from customers. The uniqueness of Paris Cleaners was its operation—many of its customers never actually visited the cleaners. Williams had more employees on his payroll than any other African American–owned business in the city.

Paris Cleaners was not without its competitors, however. On Farish Street alone were several other cleaners owned by African Americans. There was

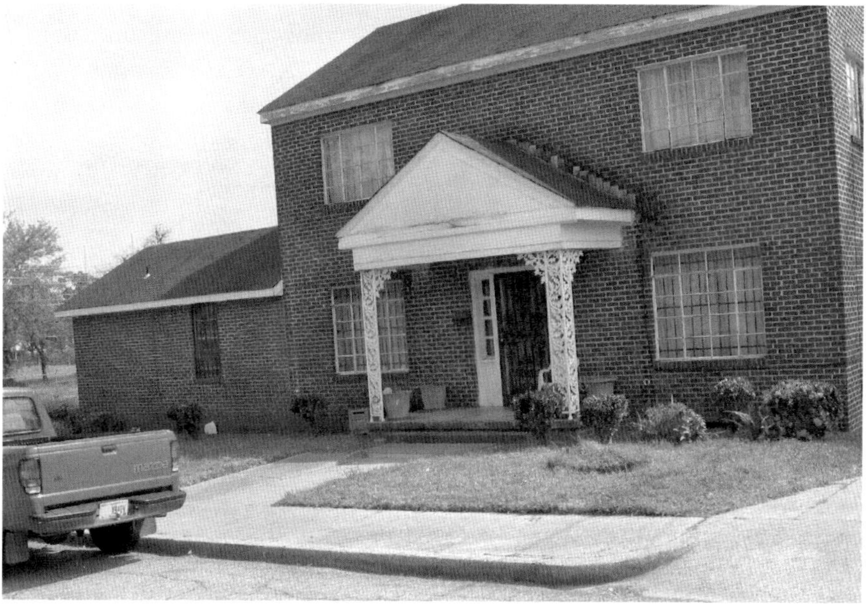

The Williams residence at 339 Church Street.

Mims Cleaners, located in the 400 block of Farish Street; Safeway Cleaners, located in the 600 block of Farish Street; and Key's Cleaners, located on Lamar Street. However, the biggest threat to the Paris Cleaners was the white-owned Crescent Laundry, located in the 700 block of Farish Street. Crescent Laundry also employed a number of African Americans.

Recently, the Paris Cleaners building was renamed the Jesse Williams building, in honor of the former owner. The building is now owned by Raybon Smith, a white male, of New Deal Grocery.

Dr. R.O. Williams was also a realtor. He owned a two-story building located at 603 North Farish Street, where he later relocated his office. The reason Dr. Williams relocated his office to this building has to do with a murder that occurred in the Paris Cleaners building, which was also home to several apartments. It appears that one of the apartment occupants was shot by an unknown assailant and died. Apparently, it took a long time to ascertain where the stench that filled the air was coming from. But even after removing the cadaver, the "foul odor" remained. Dr. Williams therefore moved into the building he owned.

Dr. Williams relocated to 603 North Farish Street in the late 1940s. This building was located next door to the Hollywood Hotel, which was owned by African American realtor Fred Scott. Next to the Hollywood Hotel were the Dotson Barber Shop and Oliver's Variety Shop. Directly in front of 603 North Farish Street was the fabulous Crystal Palace, and across the street was the Ritz Theater, owned by Dr. McCoy. Shepherd Kitchenette, the classy African American restaurant owned by David D. Shepherd, was located next to the Ritz Theater. In later years, Shepherd Kitchenette and the Ritz Theater were torn down, and the beautiful Stevens Kitchen was built by Mr. Willie Stevens, who also owned the famous Stevens Rose Room, located in Hinds County.

The building at 603 North Farish Street was uniquely designed. Although there was no basement, the building was at least five feet off the ground. There was a front porch on both the first and second floors. The steps leading to the first floor were made of concrete and were used by many Farish Streeters as "bleachers," especially when a parade was passing by.

Like the other African American doctors of the period, Dr. Williams was an astute realtor. His medical practice was on the first floor of his building. Also on the first floor, he rented space that served as the headquarters of the Negro YMCA. Upstairs, he rented space to the Johnson School of Business that Duke and Nellie Williams operated. When the Johnson School of Business closed in the 1940s, half of the second floor was rented to the Negro division of the *Clarion-Ledger*. Later, Mississippi Publishers purchased the *Jackson Daily News*, and the Negro division of that paper moved in with the Negro *Clarion-Ledger*. Lawrence Hayes, Oscar White and Clarence Johnson (all African Americans) were the managers of these Negro divisions of the two newspapers. In the early 1960s, Dr. Williams rented the other half of the second floor to the first Legal Services in Jackson, Mississippi. Dr. Williams had a full complement of renters until 1969, when Legal Services closed its office and Mississippi Publishers moved the *Clarion-Ledger/Jackson Daily News* offices to its main headquarters on Pearl Street.

Dr. Williams was fond of his Ford Mustang, but in the 1970s, a freak accident paralyzed him from the waist down. Thinking that his Mustang was in drive when it was actually in reverse, he crashed into a building. Dr. Williams was confined to his home on Church Street for several months until Dr. Aaron Shirley of the Hinds County Comprehensive Health Center hired him. He retired and subsequently died.

The Farish Street Baptist Church purchased Dr. Williams's building and the Conic Supply building, demolishing them both and extending its parking lot.

Dr. R.O. Williams was a polished gentleman and a stylish dresser. He was also a very private man. This may explain why no information on him appeared on the Internet or in the two leading African American newspapers. There was no information about Dr. Williams in the Mississippi Department of Archives and History records, nor was there any information contained in the open files of the Mississippi Sovereignty Commission. It is believed that Dr. Williams was spared scrutiny by the Sovereignty Commission because one of his renters was Mississippi Publishers. At the same time, the Legal Services office in his building also escaped the watchful eye of the spy agency.

Dr. Williams also loved poker. On the weekends, he usually joined the poker game held in George Harmon's drugstore in the Crystal Palace building. The poker games were exclusive, and regulars included Nolan Tate (Fuller Product), John Jones (Security Life Insurance Company), Dr. R.O. Williams and Dr. George Harmon.

Dr. Williams was a man of habit. He always entered his office from the back door of his building. He also made house calls until the day he became paralyzed, as most of his patients were older adults. Dr. Williams died on June 20, 1984.

Willie Stevens also had a restaurant directly in front of Dr. Williams's building. Stevens Kitchen, in the 1960s, was considered a safe haven for the freedom riders and other civil rights workers. Accordingly, many dignitaries were in and out of the restaurant at all times of the day. It was not unusual for Aaron Henry, Charles Evers, Martin Luther King Jr., Robert Kennedy, Little Willie John, B.B. King or Reverend Abernathy to be seen leaving or going into Stevens Kitchen. Many African Americans spent hours watching the front entrance of Stevens from the steps of Dr. Williams's building.

When a picture of the old Stevens Kitchen was taken on September 24, 2011, there was a distinguished looking African American standing near. The gentleman said that he had been a barber on Farish Street for many years and that he was eighty-six years old. His conversation centered on the good times at the old Stevens Kitchen. The retired barber said, "It does not matter that the building is battered and torn—it still looks good to me." He expressed sweet memories of Stevens Kitchen. In his mind, he said that he could visualize:

- Sister Sarah Harvey Stevens, the editor of the *Mississippi Enterprise*, typing her editorial at a table in front of the jukebox. Her typing was in tune with the music.
- Brother MacNeaman, Sarah Harvey's father, having the coffee ready for the early 5:00 a.m. customers.
- The famous Little Willie John playing the jukebox and dancing.

- Willie Miller, the publisher of the *Mississippi Enterprise*, serving himself coffee.
- Percy Greene, publisher of the *Jackson Advocate*, eating a steak, still frying, served on a silver platter.
- A barber from the barbershop next door checking out the place several times a day for good-looking young chicks.
- A Doty Cab driver with his head in door, hollering, "Anyone called a cab?"
- Martin Luther King Jr. having lunch.
- The safe house for the 1961 Freedom Riders. They could relax in Stevens.
- Alice Walker, author of *The Color Purple*, pregnant with her first child.
- His co-worker from the barbershop never paying for his coffee.
- The Staple Singers making Stevens Kitchen their headquarters while being stranded in Jackson for several weeks.
- The back of Robert Kennedy as he was leaving.

Those were the good old days, and Dr. R.O. Williams was one of the main players.

Chapter 11

Evangeline Byrd

Mrs. Evangeline Byrd, known as the "Midwife of Church Street" in the early days, was born on March 3, 1889. Her parents were Jimmie Rodgers and Charla Frazier. Mrs. Byrd lived at 241 Church Street for many years. Her home was located near the homes of the Williams and Redmond families on the hill of Church Street, and across the street were the homes of the Perkins and Conic families. Mrs. Byrd's husband died early in their marriage, thus making her a widow many years before her death.

Mrs. Byrd's home had a front porch that extended from one end of the house to the other. She had two roomers, Mrs. Beulah and her husband, and the three spent a lot of time on the front porch drinking homemade lemonade. They never missed a chance to speak to anyone passing by the house.

However, Mrs. Byrd kept a watchful eye from her front porch on the activities taking place in neighborhood. The young folks often said that Mrs. Byrd was "nosey" and "could see around corners." One thing was for certain: Mrs. Byrd was going to tell the parents of neighborhood kids involved in any suspected wrongdoings. She gave more advice than "Dear Abbey."

Evangeline Byrd was a tall, attractive lady that walked as if she was the Queen of Sheba and dressed as if she was Florence Nightingale. She was always dressed in a starched white dress, white stockings and white shoes. However, on Sunday, her attire changed, as she was dressed to the hilt in beautiful organza dresses and a wide straw hat during the summer months. She dressed in tailored suits and pin-box hats during the fall season.

The white outfits were her work clothes, and even though Mrs. Byrd was not formally trained, she played her part well as being the nurse and midwife for the families in the neighborhood. The community regularly called on her service. It is believed that she received her midwife gift, mother wit and folk remedies for women's care from her ancestors, because in Jackson at this time in history, there were no training facilities for African American females in this particular field.

Evangeline Byrd did not drive an automobile; she walked to most of her required destinations. Her service as a midwife was needed by the neighborhood and nearby communities both day and night. Although she worked closely with several local doctors, she often completed the delivery of babies unassisted. Many times, the women served by Mrs. Byrd never visited a hospital. There were, however, two hospitals owned by African American doctors at the time. Dr. O.I. Smith owned the Sallie Harris Clinic on North Farish Street near the Crystal Palace building, and Dr. C.B. Christian owned the Jefferson Memorial Hospital on North Farish Street near Simon Grocery and the First Street Café. Ironically, Dr. Smith's home was across the street from the Jefferson Memorial Hospital. Finally, there was one public hospital available to Mrs. Byrd's patients—Charity Hospital on the corner of Fortification and State Streets. Charity Hospital later became the University Medical Center.

In time, Mrs. Byrd gained a respectable reputation as a midwife. In 1947, midwives attended to 36 percent of the 23,815 women who bore children in Mississippi. Seldom did African American women receive physician care. Their medical care was provided by the African American midwife, who sometimes spent days in their home. The State of Mississippi required midwives to be licensed; however, no state official bothered to check for a license, especially among the small number of African American midwives. Over the years, Mrs. Evangeline Byrd delivered a countless number of babies.

Evangeline Byrd was a staunch member of Central United Methodist Church, having worked with many of the early pastors—men of the gospel such as Beverly T. McEwen, Amos L. Holland, J.W.E. Bowen Jr., A.B. Keeling, J.D. Wheaton, S.L. Webb, D.M. Ray, E.A. Mays and Wendell P.C. Taylor. Mrs. Byrd also worked on committees with some well-known sisters of the church, including Betty Marino, Sallie Reynolds, Sally Hudson and Mary Collins.

History has been kind to Mrs. Evangeline Byrd. A lady with no record of a formal education in midwifery or in any other medical field has excelled.

She was intelligent and well respected as a midwife and admired by people from all walks of life. It is simply amazing how Church Street in the early days produced these wonderful people.

Evangeline Byrd often visited her children, William Byrd and Ola Williams Byrd Murihead, in Chicago. While in Chicago, she visited museums and expositions and, of course, was extended many social courtesies. Her daughter, Ola, was a socialite in the Chicago area. Ola's mother groomed and primed her for the position that she held with the social skills that had been instilled. The sky was the limit for Ola.

Evangeline Byrd died on December 30, 1972, at the age of eighty-three. She was buried in the Greenwood Cemetery on Lamar Street. The historic Greenwood Cemetery was established January 1, 1823, by an act of the Mississippi State Legislature. It has expanded from the six acres originally designated for the cemetery to its present twenty-two acres. Greenwood is the final resting place of seven governors of Mississippi, members of the clergy, educators, civic leaders, veterans and ordinary citizens. Until the end of the nineteenth century, all Jacksonians—white, black, slave, master—were buried here. Greenwood has remained integrated, and both black and white burials still occur here.

Unit 2

Other Great Individuals

Chapter 12

The Good Citizens of Church Street

Other Families of Church Street

There were other families, of course, that lived on Church Street during the early days. These were not high-profile families, and stories about the members were not featured in the *Jackson Advocate* or the *Mississippi Enterprise* newspapers. They were simply good citizens living in a segregated society who, in the tradition of those wonderful African American citizens of Church Street, earned a living, owned property and educated their children. Everyone that lived on Church Street during the early days either worked or attended school. There was no "loafing," nor was there any crime.

Sally Hudson

Sally Hudson was born in 1870. The 1930 United States Federal Census shows that she lived at 232 East Church Street and was the head of the household. After her husband died in 1930, she took in three male boarders for supplemental income. She was an active member of the Central United Methodist Church and involved in many church activities.

Prior to her move to Church Street, Mrs. Hudson owned a house on North Farish Street, directly across from Central United Methodist Church. Mrs. Collins of Collins Funeral Home, a good friend, negotiated a deal

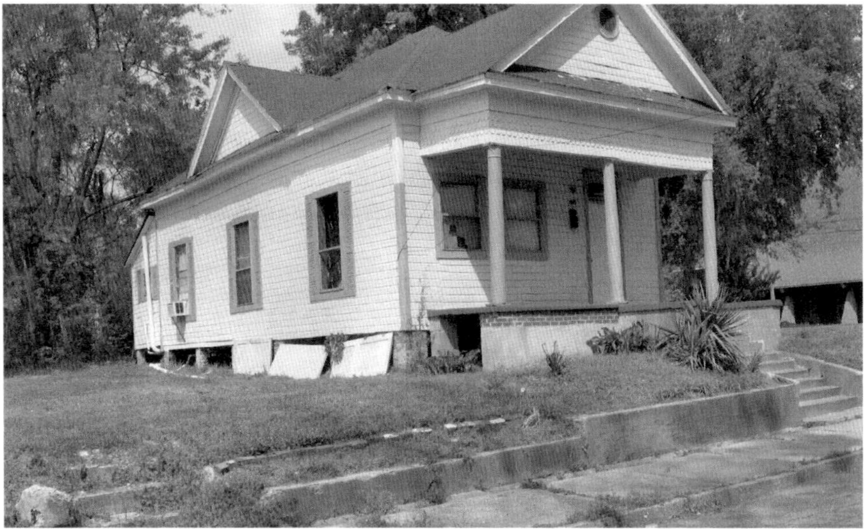

Sally Hudson's home.

with Mrs. Hudson for her property on North Farish Street. Collins Funeral Home is currently located on the lot where the Hudsons' home once stood. In exchange, Mrs. Collins gave Mrs. Hudson the house located at 232 East Church Street.

Previously, Collins Funeral Home was located on the other side of Farish Street, in a smaller location near Home Dining Room Café. The funeral home needed to expand, and the Hudson property afforded the opportunity for this expansion. When Sally Hudson died, the house at 232 Church Street was retained by Collins Funeral Home.

Bernard Wade

Bernard Wade was hired by Collins Funeral Home in the early 1940s and eventually achieved the position of director. He became an important man around town, serving on many social committees and holding several positions with the L.K. Atwood Elk's Lodge. His father was also a well-known individual around town, having lived in west Jackson and served for many years as manager of the Booker T. Theater on the 100 block of Farish Street. Leroy Jackson, who was already the manager of the Alamo Theater on Amite Street, assumed the managerial position at the Booker T. Theater when Bernard's father retired.

Bernard Wade lived at 232 East Church Street in the former home of Sally Hudson. He secured this home from his employer, Mrs. Collins. In some circles, it is believed the house was a gift from the funeral home. Bernard Wade served as the funeral home's director for many years. Eventually, Mrs. Collins's daughter, Claire Collins Harvey, became the major player in the management of the funeral home. Bernard Wade retired and joined his wife and several children in New Orleans. For a second time, the house located at 232 East Church Street became the property of Collins Funeral Home.

JOHN GARRNETT

John Garrnett was born on December 25, 1922, to Aaron Garrnett and Mary Redmond. Garrnett was a photographer, and his studio was located in the 500 block of North Farish Street, next door to the headquarters of the Black and Tan Republican Party. In the mid-1950s, Garrnett moved his studio to a new brick building next door to Farish Street Baptist Church—the same building that later became the home of Conic Beauty and Supply and Johnson Lock and Key.

For many years, Richard H. Beadle had been the premier photographer in Jackson. John Garrnett became a serious competitor. At this time, there was one other African American photographer in the city, a freelancer named Hunter. Mr. Hunter worked out of his home on North Lamar Street near Fortification Street.

John Garrnett married one of Mr. Sims's daughters, Edna, who lived on East Church Street. John Garrnett and his bride lived at 232 Church, the same house once owned by Sally Hudson and later occupied by Bernard Wade. John and Edna were the parents of two boys and one girl.

John Garrnett died on November 23, 1965.

ALBERT BUTANE

Albert Butane was a successful plasterer by trade. He owned a huge two-story building located at 136 Church Street. The house was divided into four

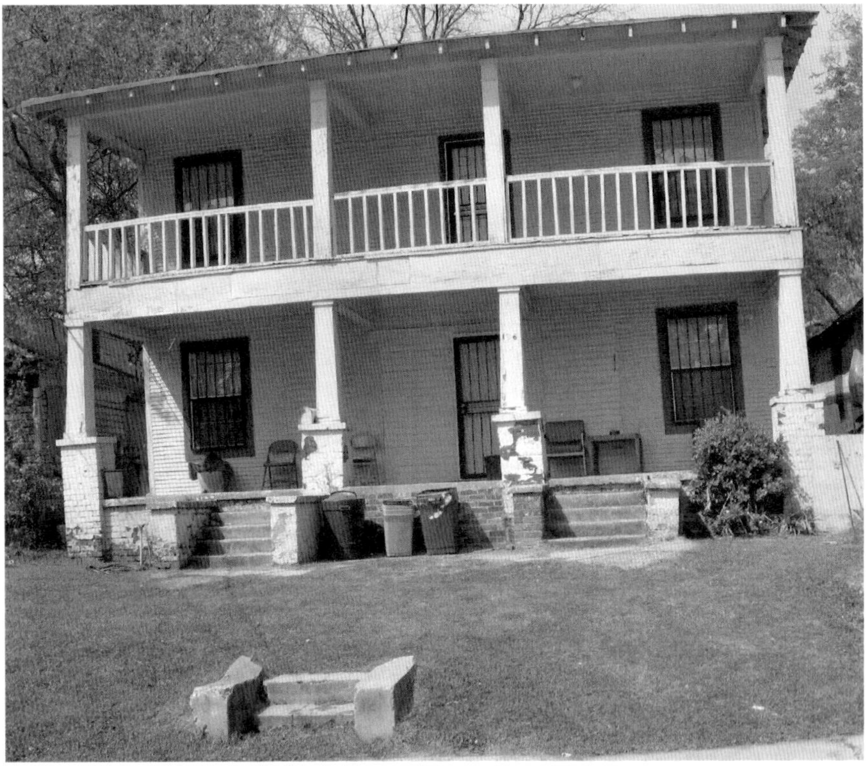

Mr. Brittain's house, one of the first two-story homes in the neighborhood, is still standing.

apartments. He lived in one of the apartments on the first floor. He had no problem renting the apartments because they were the best in the city.

Albert Butane was the first African American landlord to introduce the apartment lifestyle to the African American community in the late 1930s. Although he maintained that he was an African American, he had characteristics similar to people from the Middle East and a slight telltale accent.

African American plasterers were well paid during the early days of Church Street. Therefore, many successful African Americans in Jackson were once plasterers. Willie Stevens of Stevens Rose Room was a plasterer. W.A. Summers, the owner of Summers Hotel and the Blackstone Café, was also a plasterer. The debonair Ferdinand Moore was a plasterer, as was I.J. Head. Louis Turner Jr., an early trustee of Central United Methodist Church, was a plaster and played a major role in unionizing the African American plasterers of Jackson.

ELBERT TOPP JR.

Elbert Topp Jr., born on January 21, 1896, was the son of Reverend Elbert Topp Sr., who organized the Farish Street Baptist Church. His mother was the former Miss Carrie Collier. In the early days of his life, Elbert moved to Chicago for employment. He held several menial jobs until he became the chauffeur for a well-known Chicago gangster, Frank Nitti. He returned to Mississippi shortly after Nitti committed suicide. Elbert and his partner, Massey Hawkins, once owned the popular Tip Top Nite Club. This club was located on Whitfield Mills Road.

Elbert Topp Jr. returned to the family home on East Church Street. He renovated the house and married Jessie, who was related to Mrs. Collins of Collins Funeral Home. He became a popular doorman and bartender at the Patio Club located on Lamar Street, next door to the Sun-n-Sand Motel. The Patio Club was a private white club owned by Mr. Barfield of Barfield Office Furniture Company.

Elbert Topp Jr. died on June 18, 1977. His wife, Jessie, worked many years at Collins Funeral Home before she died.

PERCY ABRAMS

Percy Abrams lived on West Church Street in the early 1930s. Like most of the homes on Church Street, his was a beautiful home with hardwood floors and a modern kitchen. Abrams was employed by the Universal Life Insurance Company of Memphis, Tennessee. The Abrams had two children who attended the neighborhood schools.

After living in Jackson for several years, Percy Abrams moved to Los Angeles, California, and became a successful insurance agent. He sold his home to Dr. A.B. Britton Jr. in 1951. The Britton family remained on Church Street until 1957, when they moved to their new, modern home at 1510 Whitfield Mills Road.

GEORGE BRACEY

George Bracey, a longtime driver for Doty Cab, lived at 112 Church Street. He rented one of the shotgun houses owned by a white merchant in the area. In the early days of Church Street, Doty Cab drivers were held in high esteem. Willard Johnson, an African American, always kept new cars in his fleet. Cab drivers with a good reputation were known to earn a decent living.

The Doty Cab Company had several legendary cab drivers, including "Cold Milk" and "Shorty George" of West Church Street and "Wild Daddy" and George Bracey of Church Street. They earned more than African American schoolteachers, preachers and some lawyers. It was not unusual for the four cab drivers mentioned to earn $100 or more per week. George Bracey was the perfect gentleman and reliable at all times; however, the other three drivers mentioned were considered flamboyant and trash talkers. Seldom did George Bracey miss work due to sickness or other reasons.

Bracey had several children, including one daughter who attended college.

CICERO LEE

Cicero Lee and his wife, Eula Solomon Lee, lived at 114 West Church Street. Cicero was a cook employed by the Illinois Central Railroad whose job required him to spend many days away from home. Eula Lee was a housewife and maintained the family while he was away. The Lees were the parents of four children, one boy and three girls. One of the girls, Annie Kay, became a teacher, and Henry Lee, the only boy, was a longtime employee of an electronics company in Chicago. He retired early and returned to Jackson to live with his mother. Cicero Lee died in the late 1950s. Directly across the street from the Lees' home was Bubble Grocery, a thriving business. James Solomon, Mrs. Eula Lee's brother, was the proprietor of Bubble Grocery. Mrs. Bert Rundles, the mother of James Rundle, was the Lees' next-door neighbor.

ELMA SENTHIA SLAUGHTER

Elma Slaughter lived at 134 East Church Street. She grew up and attended school in the Tougaloo community, graduating from Tougaloo College in 1926.

Elma Slaughter was an instructor at Smith Robertson Elementary School for many years. A strict disciplinarian, she was always assigned to teach the

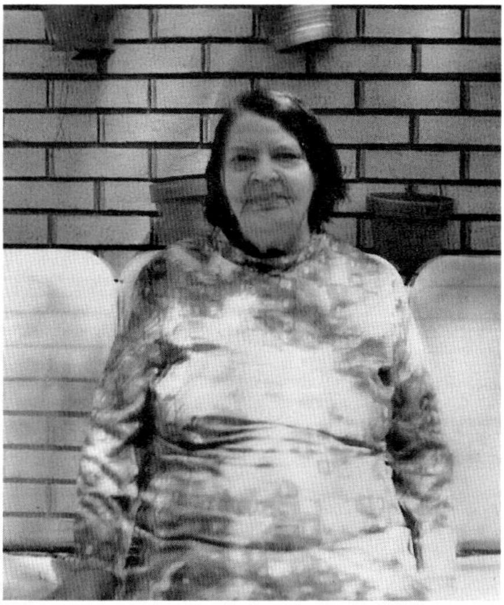

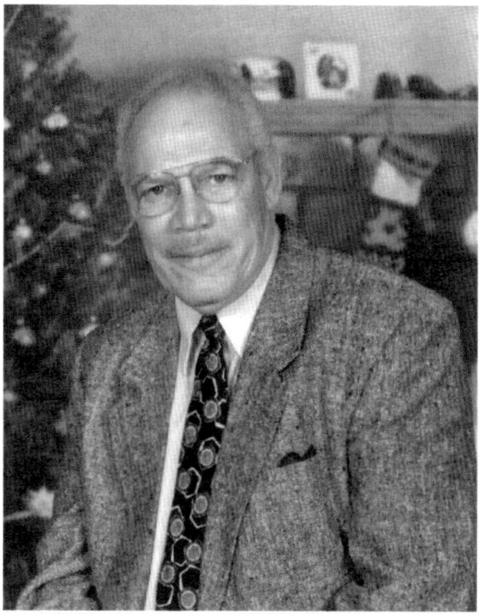

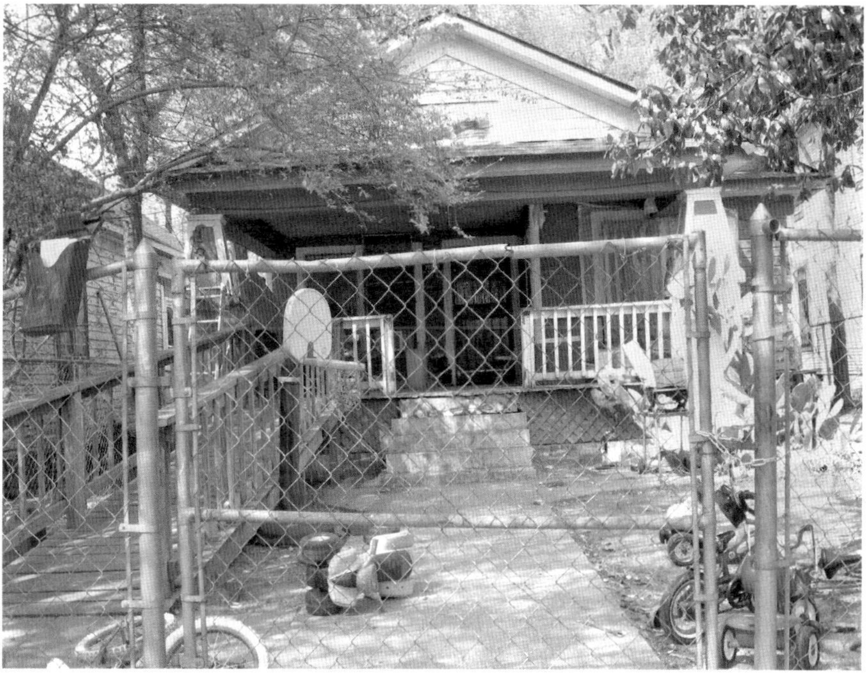

Top, left: Mrs. Elma Slaughter.

Top, right: Elijah Slaughter.

Bottom: The Slaughter house, located at 134 East Church Street. The house was built by Jim Slaughter, a local contractor. Ernest H. Slaughter was the owner. Both men were the brothers of Elma Slaughter.

third grade. Elma Slaughter ended her long career as a teacher at Brown's Elementary School on Ash Street.

Emma Slaughter eventually relocated to Wiggin Street, in west Jackson, with her new husband, Mr. Harper. She was a coworker of Gladys Noel Bates in 1947 and during her career worked under the supervision of three principals: Professors Dabney, Wilson and Jackson.

The house at 134 Church Street is rich in African American history. The home's first occupant was Walter "Duke" Williams, who rented the house. Williams stayed at 134 East Church until his beautiful home on the upper end of East Church was completed. Jim Slaughter, the contractor of the new home, was married to Anna Farish. Farish Street was named in honor of his wife's family.

Ernest Slaughter was one of the first African American postmen hired in the city of Jackson. His family included seven children. All of the Slaughter children completed college. The Slaughter family is highly respected in and around the Tougaloo community.

Elijah Slaughter, Elma's nephew, is a staunch supporter of Tougaloo College and the historian of the Slaughter family.

BERTHA BEATRICE KING RUNDLES

Bertha Beatrice King Rundles was born in Hermanville, Mississippi. The exact date of her birth is unknown; however, records indicate that she was born around the 1890s and at an early age met and married James Isaiah Rundles. James Rundles was a minister and was born in Liberia, today officially known as the Republic of Liberia. This union produced one daughter and four sons.

Records indicate that James Rundles Sr. died around 1930. At that time, his youngest child was just two years old. Bertha Rundles found herself with the responsibility of being both mother and father to her four boys: Samuel, James Jr., Paul and Joel, the baby of the family. Ruth Viola Rundles was the only girl in the family.

Bertha Rundles lived on West Church Street during the late 1930s. Her next-door neighbor was Cicero Lee. She also lived across the street from the Percy Abrams house, which was later purchased by Dr. A.B. Britton Jr.

All four of the Rundles boys enlisted or were drafted into the U.S. Armed Forces at the beginning of World War II. James Jr. volunteered for the U.S.

Marines, becoming the first African American from Jackson to serve in that force. He was followed into the Marines by his brother Paul, who also went on to serve in the United States Army. Samuel was drafted into the U.S. Army, and Joel joined the United States Army near the time of the Korean Conflict. All of the Rundles boys were honorably discharged with decorations for bravery.

James Jr. became somewhat of a celebrity around the city of Jackson. He married a beautiful nurse named Mattie, who became the first African American supervisor of a nursing staff at the Veteran Administration Hospital in Mississippi. Mattie also owned and operated a haberdashery that was located in the Jesse Williams building.

Unit 3

Reflections

Reminiscing

Reminiscence refers to recollections of memories from the past. It is familiar to us all and can be utilized for the benefit of others, namely, the readers. Accordingly, we were fortunate to get several individuals who grew up on Church Street to share their precious memories of this magical street.

Chapter 13

Annie Rose Wheaton Walker

Reverend James D. Wheaton, my father, moved to Jackson from Meridian, Mississippi, around 1944, when I was six years old. He pastored at Central United Methodist Church, and I attended the fourth grade at Smith Robertson Elementary School. Professor Charles H. Wilson was the principal at that time.

Our neighborhood was well kept by mostly professional black people. There was one good-size grocery store nearby. Many black businesses were located on Farish Street—to name a few: Doty Cab, Shepherd Kitchenette, Mosley Shoe Shop, Paris Dry Cleaners, Collins Funeral Home and the Sallie Harris Clinic, which was the first African American hospital in Jackson. Dr. Smith owned the hospital. Just to mention a few influential black people who lived on Church Street: attorney Carsie Hall; Mrs. Georgia Hodge, a well-known business lady; and Dr. Redmond, who was also a lawyer and one of the first of his race to be involved in Mississippi politics.

We lived in the Church parsonage, directly behind Bob's Grocery Store, which was located on the corner of Farish and Church Streets. Edward Lee Hotel was on West Church Street a block from Farish Street Baptist Church. Across the street from Farish Street Baptist Church was Conic Barber Shop.

After leaving Smith Robertson Elementary School, I attended Jackson College Laboratory School for two years. At that time, Mr. Lee Williams was the principal. It was at Jackson College Laboratory School where I first

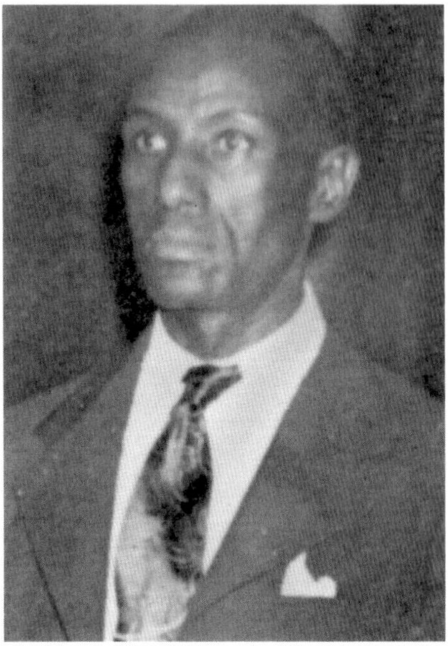

Reverend J.D. Wheaton, 1945.

met Juliet Blackburn and Mattwilda Dobbs. Mattwilda Dobbs was the sister of Juliet's mother. Shirley Reddix was also at Jackson College Laboratory School. Her father was the president of Jackson College.

Two years later, my parents transferred me to Tougaloo High School, where I stayed for two years. Miss Annie Davis was the principal. We then moved to Hattiesburg, Mississippi, where my daddy was pastor at St. Paul Methodist church for at least six years.

Although I have been away from Jackson, Mississippi, and specifically Church Street for many years, those pleasant memories are still fresh in my mind. I will never forget the time spent at my father's church, Central United Methodist. All of the important African Americans attended this church. For example, included in the membership were Dr. A.H. McCoy, Dr. Sidney Redmond, Mr. David D. Shepherd, Mrs. M.A. Collins, Dr. C.B. Christian, Mr. Burr Brown, Mrs. Willie Rudd, Mrs. Minnie Farish and Ms. Evangeline Byrd—just to name a few. In later years, I learned that some of those people, over the years, made major contributions in the history of the African Americans in Jackson.

Chapter 14
Ruby Thames Bryant

Growing up on Church Street was truly an adventure that will long be remembered. My family, consisting of three boys and two girls, was headed by my mother, Mrs. Georgia Thames, a very strong Christian woman. She moved to Jackson in the late 1940s from Decatur, Mississippi. After she established a place of residence with relatives on Oakley Street, who shared their modest home with her, she soon moved her girls, my sister Eula Mae and me into this already crowded home. My mother always sought the best that she could muster for her children. Later, she was able to move into a tiny home on John Hart Street, and my three brothers joined us. The boys, who had already dropped out of school, were older and were able to find employment to supplement her meager income.

Upon moving to Jackson, my sister and I were immediately enrolled in Smith Robertson Elementary School. Our mother was employed as custodian at the school, and needless to say, she kept a critical eye on our progress. Even though her formal education had been cut short by an early stress-filled marriage and a family of five children, she constantly stressed the importance of education to her children. The boys, by this time, were gainfully employed and were not willing to relinquish their positions to return to school.

Attending Smith Robertson was a rewarding experience for my sister and me. One thing which remains quite vivid to me was our celebration of May Day. This was a time in which every child in the school was involved in many hours of practice to perfect our dances. The girls in each class wore beautiful, colorful paper shirts, with each class using a different color. It was sometimes a chore to keep the mischievous boys from tearing the skirts just to antagonize the girls. Each class spent much time perfecting their dances to the delight of parents and people from the neighborhood. Generally, the culminating event was several classes wrapping the May Pole in concert. This activity still stands out in my memory as a part of my elementary years.

Grace Britton and I were childhood playmates and neighbors. We spent many hours entertaining ourselves playing jacks, jumping rope and making up other games, as there were few organized activities for young black children in the neighborhood. To the great surprise of my children, I never learned to ride a bicycle or to roller skate. Grace and I spent countless hours watching and interacting with children from as far away as west Jackson who often congregated on Church Street to roller skate and ride bicycles. They especially liked to skate here because of the incline on the street, which gave them momentum as they perfected their intricate maneuvers on their roller skates. Most of the girls who lived on Church Street were also involved with the Bethlehem Center, which was then housed next door to Central United Methodist Church. There we learned to embroider, crochet and do simple cooking. Our instructors included Mrs. Maggie Dunson, Mrs. Claire Collins Harvey, Ms. Minnie Farish and others whose names escape me at the moment. Ms. Minnie, as we affectionately called her, also served as our Girl Scout leader. Girl scouting played a pivotal role in my development. I vividly remember the many fun-filled times I spent at Camp Minnie Ha Ha in the area near Clinton, Mississippi. This camp was very primitive and a far cry from the present Camp Wahi, but we looked forward with eager anticipation to spending time there each summer.

One final thing as I take this sentimental journey—I remember going to the kiddie matinee at the Alamo Theater on Saturday mornings. Ms. Lula Mae Hopkins, who was also my first grade teacher, and Mr. Leroy Jackson were the driving forces behind this adventure. They always held talent shows where we were free to display our "talents" before an audience consisting of our peers, who sometimes were not so kind in their evaluation of the performances. These shows preceded the viewing of movies which the youth of today would probably find most boring. But the Church Street youngsters were there on most Saturday mornings. My childhood on Church Street was filled with many events that I will forever cherish.

Chapter 15

Benjamin Bradley

My name is Benjamin Bradley, and I was raised on Short Mill Street. My street was just one block behind North Farish Street. I attended Smith Robertson Junior High School on Bloom Street. Professor Charles H. Wilson was just replacing Professor Dabney at that time. My first grade teacher was Mrs. Stutts. My first job was with the Alamo Theater on Amite Street. The Alamo was owned by Arthur Lamon, a Jew, and Leroy Jackson, an African American, was the manager of both the Alamo and Booker T. Theaters. Bernard Wade's daddy was the assistant manager of the Booker T. Theater. At the time, I was nine years old. At the Alamo Theater, I was classified as the "popcorn boy." I sold popcorn for a nickel a bag to the patrons inside the movie. My compensation for this duty was a whopping commission of 8 percent of what I sold during the week. One time, I made $4.20. But money was not that important, because I had the ideal job—I saw all the movies, and I could even visit the Booker T. Theater for free. At this time, I was not really familiar with Church Street; however, I did know of its location.

When I reached the age of ten, I left the Alamo Theater and started a new job at a store located at 334 North Farish Street known as Silver Savers, whose motto was, "Save your silver at Silver Savers." My employers were J.E. Simon and his brother-in-law, Norman Sawaya. Both gentlemen were of Middle East origin…Syrian. My new job title was that of "grocery delivery boy." My new salary was ten dollars per week, which consisted of six days. I rode a jitterbug bicycle and delivered groceries to

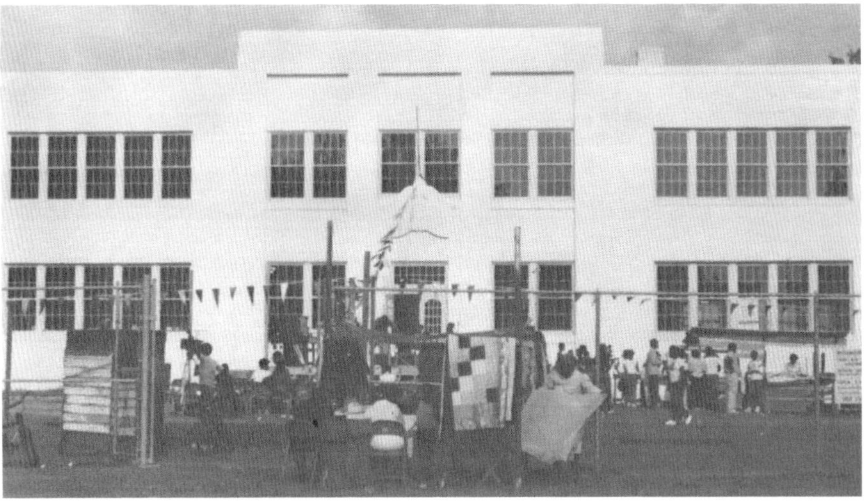

Smith Robertson School. *Courtesy of Smith Robertson Museum & Cultural Center, Jackson, Mississippi.*

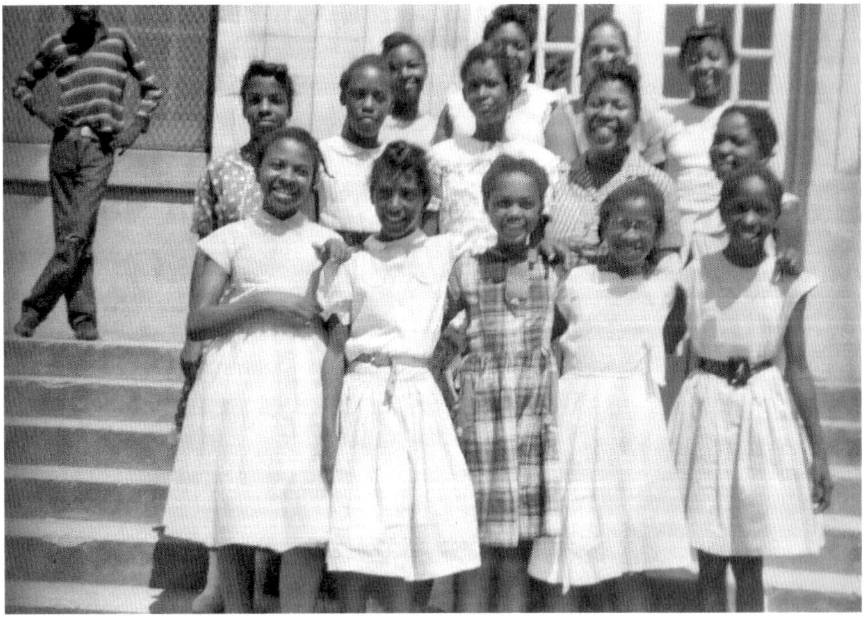

Students from the Smith Robertson School. *Courtesy of Smith Robertson Museum & Cultural Center, Jackson, Mississippi.*

customers' homes. It was at this time that I really became acquainted with Church Street, as most of my deliveries were to those beautiful homes on Church Street. I made daily deliveries to the Edward Lee Hotel, and Mr. Lee became a good friend of my Cub Scout troop. I got to know Mrs. Doris Hall and her husband, attorney Carsie Hall. Also, I knew Sidney Tharp, who was also an attorney and Mrs. Hall's brother. I knew the Williams family, who managed Security Life Insurance Company and later owned the Penguin Café. I remember Mrs. Hodge, who I believed was the richest African American woman on Church Street; Ms. Slaughter, a longtime teacher at Smith Robertson; Mr. Frank Conic, who was a barber and a businessman; Mr. Albert Butane, who was a plasterer and owned the only two-story apartment building on East Church; Professor Shinault, who oversaw the Deaf School; Dr. R.O Williams, a physician who owned a two-story building at 603 North Farish; Mr. Lee, a relative of Edward Lee and a cook on the Illinois Central Train; Miss "Babe," who ran the ice cream parlor known as Sloppy Joe's; Samuel Rundles, brother of James Rundles; Elbert Topp, the son of Reverend Topp; and George Bracey, a well-known Doty Cab driver. I was not familiar with Dr. Redmond, who did not visit the store where I worked. I knew Dr. Redmond as being the "big shot" on East Church, as Mr. Edward Lee was the "big shot" on West Church.

I remember there were some pretty girls on Church Street, but boys like me could not do much courting because they were closely supervised. There was a big field behind the home of Mrs. Doris Hall. She had this field cleared and made it available to boys my age to play softball. The older boys had taken the playground at Smith Robertson. On the holidays, I would either skate or ride my bicycle on the hill of East Church because that is where the kids would gather.

In 1949, I completed the ninth grade at Smith Robertson. I started school in September that same year at Tougaloo High School and graduated in 1953. At this time, I lost contact with Church Street—but not the memories.

Chapter 16

Grace Weakly Lee

I was born at 148 West Church Street in 1929, the elder of two children. My baby brother, Walter, was also born on Church Street. My father worked at the King Edward Hotel on Capitol Street as a bellhop, and my mother also worked at the hotel as a cook. Aunt Maggie, my mother's sister, worked as the hotel baker. The King Edward Hotel employed quite a few African Americans; however, they were only allowed to work in those traditional black jobs.

We lived peaceful lives full of love in an immaculate, clean home. I really thought my family was part of the elites that lived on Church Street. Our parents saw that we went to school at Smith Robertson and to Campbell College. My brother, Walter, attended Lanier High School. I attended Southern University in Baton Rouge, Louisiana. My brother became gainfully employed in the private sector.

Getting back to my earlier days on Church Street, we played as young kids did in those days in the front yard. Church Street was a gravel road, and very few cars traveled on it. Eventually, Church Street became the first street in an African American community to be paved in Jackson, Mississippi. There was no crime on West Church. You could leave the house key under the mat or in the mailbox. The back door was practically never locked.

I married my childhood sweetheart, Edward Lee Jr., who lived next door to me. My husband was the son of Edward Lee Sr., who owned the Edward Lee Hotel, which was also located on Church Street. Mr. Lee's hotel was the first African American hotel in Jackson.

Later, Dr. A.B. Britton Jr. moved across the street from our house. Dr. Britton purchased the Abramses' house. Dr. Britton was a welcome addition to West Church Street, and he was respected by all in the community. West Church Street now had a private doctor in its midst. East Church Street had Dr. R.O. Williams. We were moving on up!

My family attended Mount Helm Baptist Church. Reverend A.L. Rice was the pastor. He also taught at Jackson College in west Jackson.

Looking back over my life, I now realize that I had a wonderful, pleasant life while growing up on West Church. My family and my neighbors instilled strong values and ethics in me, and I did the same with my family.

Chapter 17

Grace Britton Sweet

I arrived at 234 East Church Street when I was just three weeks old, in March 1932, after my mother passed away. I lived with my mother's sisters—Rebecca "Cully," Amanda "Dutra," Elizabeth "Little Auntie" and Lucinda "Big Auntie"—and her only brother, Uncle Lewis. My mother's family had lived at 234 East Church since 1920. My aunts' husbands had passed away, and Uncle Lewis was divorced.

The homes on East Church Street had neatly mowed lawns; you walked on that beautiful green grass at your own risk! We sat on the front porch in the late evenings and enjoyed the breezes and often a glass of lemonade. I attended Christ Temple Kindergarten, the Lutheran School on Blair Street from first through eighth grades, Smith Robertson in the ninth grade and Lanier High School on Ash Street from tenth through the twelfth grades. Ruby Thames and I were best friends and spent hours together playing jacks and with our dolls.

My girlfriend Robbie lived on Bloom Street. She and I walked to Lanier High School unless it rained excessively or snowed—then her father, Mr. Frank, would drive us to school. We did not have school buses assigned to African American schools, and we did not ride the city bus because we did not like being required to sit in the back—even if the city bus was empty. Our first ride on the city bus was our last ride. We walked to school and pocketed our dimes and used our money for the movies and candy. Robbie and I attended Sunday school at Central United Methodist Church, as well as the eleven o'clock services after Sunday school. She was the pianist

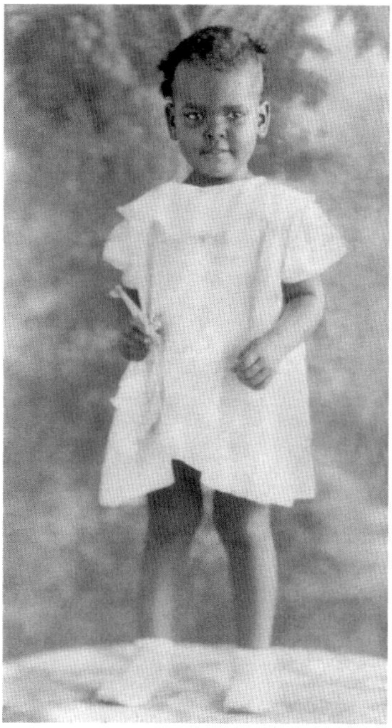

Grace Britton Sweet as a young child.

for the earlier service. Between Sunday school and church, we would walk down to Sloppy Joe's and treat ourselves to a cone of delicious ice cream custard.

Claire Collins Harvey was my godmother. Robbie and I just loved looking at her, especially when she came home from Spelman College to work at her family's funeral home. During the summer, she dressed in her fine attire. She wore floral-print dresses and wide-brim designer hats that matched her shoes and bags. Her family owned the Collins Funeral Home on North Farish Street. She was a faithful member of Central United Methodist Church.

My "Big Auntie" was so good to me. She indulged me in my love of clothes. We could not try on clothes at the stores in downtown Jackson; therefore, she would order my clothes from Sears and Roebuck or have them made by Miss Buchannon, the neighborhood seamstress. My love of clothes almost got Robbie and me in trouble.

One day when Robbie and I were about thirteen, we were looking at clothes in a store on Capitol Street when the sales clerk asked, "Can I help you, girls?" We told her, "No, we were just looking." She said, "You are supposed to say, 'No, Ma'am.'" Robbie said, "We were not taught to say No, Ma'am,'" and it was not in our schoolbooks. The clerk said, "Oh! You are not going to say, 'Yes, Ma'am' or 'No, Ma'am'?!" and then she called the police. We took off and ran home. We felt safe when we got to Church Street. We could not tell the grown-ups because they told us never to go in the stores without a grown-up.

I can remember when Church Street became the first paved street in an African American community in Jackson. That Christmas, the children came from all over town to skate on the newly paved street. Boy—what a sight to see! It was such a happy time for all the kids. Robbie, Ruby and I sat on the front porch and watched because our parents were afraid we would get hurt. Watching was fun, too.

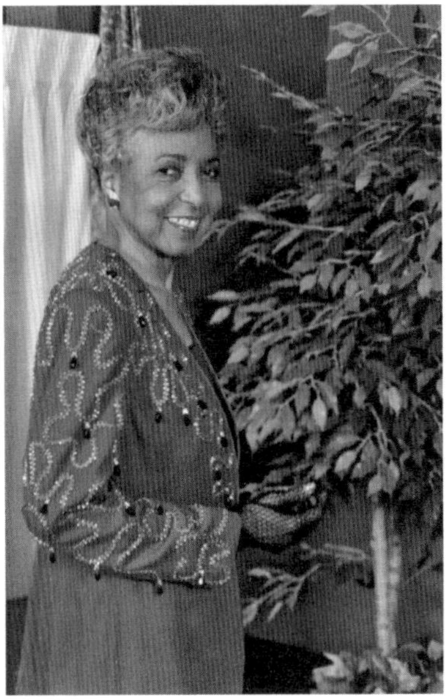

Claire Collins Harvey, owner of Collins Funeral home and godmother of Grace Sweet.

My brother Albert was ten years older than me, and he spent lots of time at school on the football team and baseball team and studying. I was so happy when my sister Lucille came to stay with us and attended stenography school. She was only three years older than me; therefore, we spent lots of time with each other. When Lucille graduated from business school, she went to the employment office and applied for a secretarial job. She was told, "We don't have any job openings for black girls, so you know we can't use you." Lucille decided to go to Chicago to live with my brother Morris, who settled there when he was discharged from the army. Lucille worked at Loop Junior College in Chicago as a secretary.

One neighbor I learned to love and never forgot was Mrs. Evangeline Byrd. Mrs. Byrd lived across the street from us. She was a tall, beautiful woman who gave me gifts on birthdays, Christmas and graduations. She was very nosey, too. One day, two boys walked Robbie and me as far the Conic's home, which was at the corner of Church and Blair. They gave us our books, and we turned the corner to go up East Church Street. It was impossible (we thought) for anyone to see them from the houses east of the Conics. However, when I arrived home, Big Auntie wanted to know who had walked home with us. Then we knew that Mrs. Byrd could see around corners.

"Mrs. Pinkie" lived behind us on Dreyfus Street, and her backyard would have joined ours if there had not been the alleyway for the garbage truck to pick up the trash. She washed and ironed clothes for a living. I used to listen to her sing as she worked. I loved her beautiful voice. Our backyard consisted of a vegetable garden, flower garden and chickens.

Mr. Bell lived farther east on Church Street and would pass our house on Friday evenings, somewhat tipsy. He would give Robbie and me a quarter most Fridays until Big Auntie saw him, and then we were told, in no uncertain terms, that we were never to take money from any male again.

At Christmastime, everyone had some sort of decoration, even if it was only a handmade wreath. We had a telephone because Uncle Lewis had to get his calls for his plumbing business. We had indoor toilets because of Uncle Lewis's plumbing business. I was about three years old when we first got gas piped into our home. Before, we had fireplaces and wooden stoves. We also had an icebox, and the iceman came by once weekly in the winter and twice weekly in the summer.

I remember the merchants that came by our house. There was "Hot Tamale Joe," with his push cart; the "Sassafras Tea Man," Dr. Seth, with strings of tea hanging around his neck; the "Snow Ball Man," on his specially constructed bicycle; and, of course, the iceman, Mr. Bowlegs from the Pete Ice Company.

Dr. Sidney Dellon Redmond lived across the street, in front of our house on Church Street. I remember that he had a maid, a yard man and a chauffeur. Dr. Redmond would always walk to his office in the 100 block of Farish Street. We knew that he was very wealthy and one of the pillars of the community. When Dr. Redmond died in 1948, I was a senior in high school. Mrs. Redmond got permission for me to spend nights with her because she was afraid to stay alone. I enjoyed the time spent with her. She always had her housekeeper cook my favorite dessert. She and I read and talked about the daily news just like Big Auntie did before she passed away in July 1947.

Mrs. Redmond wanted to send me, all expenses paid, to Rust College, but my family said no because Papa had left my college expenses in the bank for me to attend Tougaloo College or Howard University, where my brother Albert had finished medical school.

Chapter 18
Ruth Williams

Church Street was the perfect place to have a wonderful childhood. My fondest memories include playing hide-and-seek on summer evenings in the vacant lot across from my parent's home. We would catch fireflies in jars and make earrings and bracelets from them. I remember walking to town with my mother with her umbrella. It would be so hot that I would sometimes get a nosebleed on the way back, and then we would stop at Mrs. Doris Tharp Hall's house so I could cool down.

Also during the summer, one of my friends and I would lay out in one of the neighbors' gardens and eat her fresh tomatoes until she would run us home. Of course, by the time we got home, our parents would know what we had been up to, and we would be punished, usually with a spanking. My friends and I would also play in the Greenwood Cemetery, which was located at the end of the street. We would read the grave markers and play tag. On most Saturdays, the family would go to the Seale Lilly Ice Cream Parlor for a special treat. This shop was managed by Mr. Cleave Johnson, and he made the very best orange chill drink—it would give you a brain freeze! Mrs. Cora Lee worked with Mr. Cleave Johnson. She was married to the leader of the Five Blind Boys, a popular gospel group.

There were several older girls in the neighborhood who would sometimes allow me go to the movies with them. There were three movie theaters in walking distance: Alamo, Amite and Booker T. We would stop at "Big John's" [Big Apple Inn] *and pick up sandwiches, and then we would stop at the Acme Bakery and purchase a slice of cake on the way to the movie. This would be our snack. Going home, we would buy ice cream at the "Slop House"* [Cook Frozen Custard]. *There was a shop on Farish Street named the Trade Center, a drugstore with all types of items from toys to housewares. This would also be one of our stops on the way home. Going to the movies and making the side trips was always great fun. One Christmas season, the Trade Center had a black doll named Cynthia in the display window. That was the first time I had seen a black doll. I would go to visit Cynthia every chance I could and tell my parents how much I wanted that doll. On Christmas morning, Cynthia was under the Christmas tree. That was one of many wonderful Christmases that I remember.*

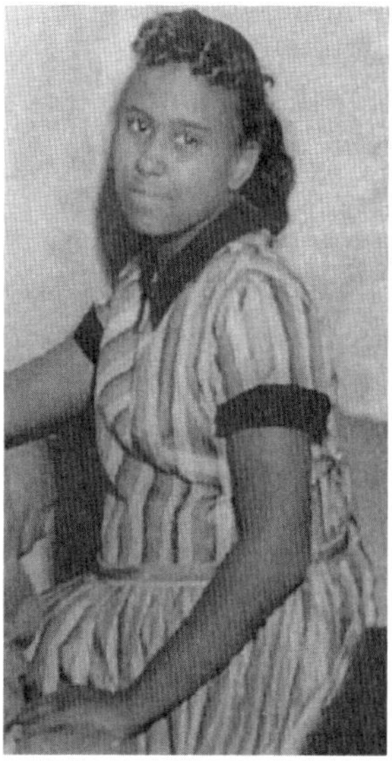

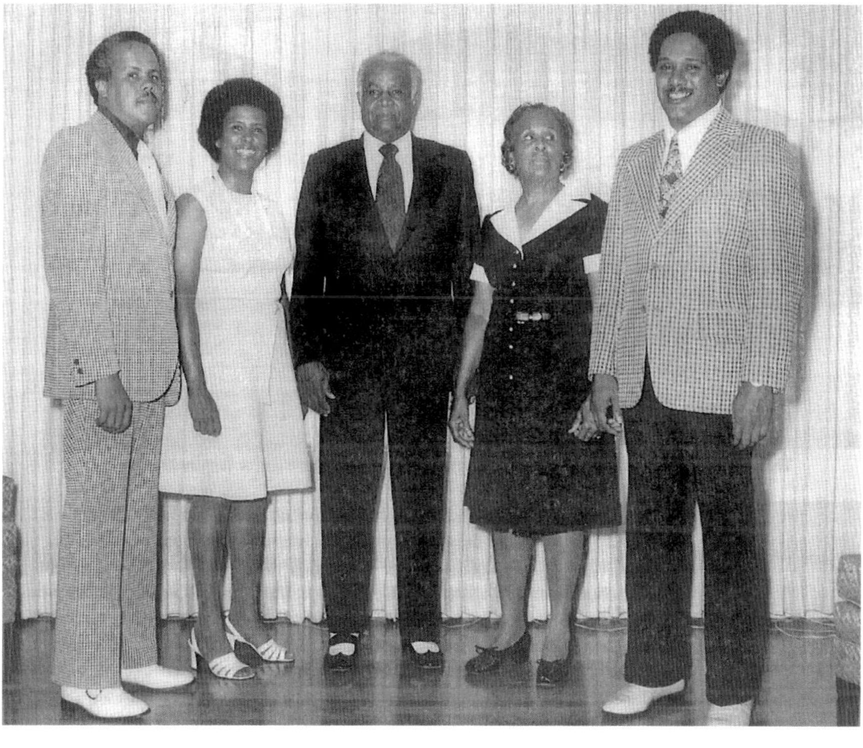

Top: Ruth Williams, age nine.

Bottom: The Williams family. *From left to right*: Walter Jr., Ruth, Walter Sr., Nellie and Byron.

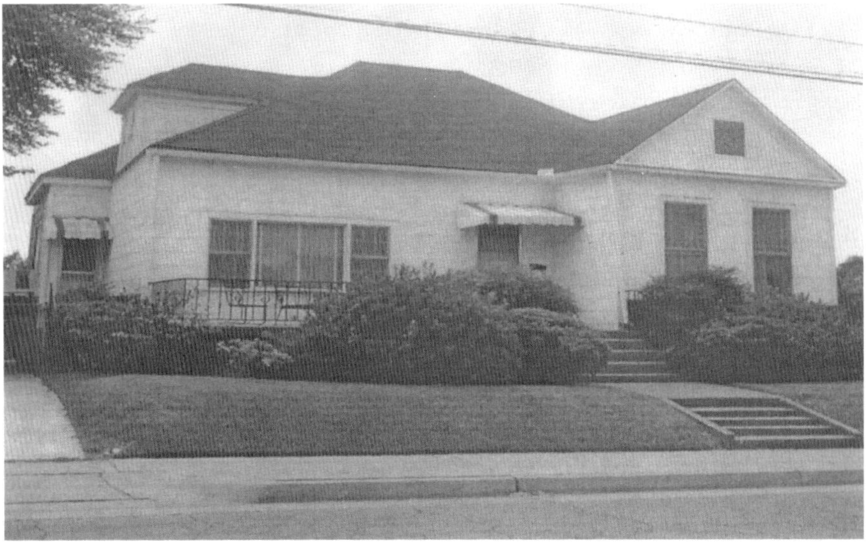

The Williams home at 223 Church Street, circa early 1950s.

My family attended Central United Methodist Church on Farish Street. Most Sundays after Sunday school, the children in my class would go to visit Mrs. Mary A. Collins, owner of the Collins Funeral Home, across from the church. Mrs. Collins would greet us at the door, and we would ask who had died that week. If we wanted to, we could view the persons, and of course we would sign every guest book. After the "viewings," we would have cookies and punch with Mrs. Collins; then we would move on to Big John's for a sandwich before going back to church service with our parents. Other Sundays, we would go to the Slop House for ice cream. Sunday was also the day my family would go for a ride after dinner. These excursions would take us to Tougaloo College or in town to visit family friends or just drive around town and the surrounding communities. This was a special time.

My brothers were older and had a lot more freedom in the neighborhood. They would walk to the Pearl River to swim and play around the state capitol until they would get run off by the security officers. Mostly, they would climb the trees and roll on the lawns. The family rule for my brothers was that they were required to be home before 6:00 p.m. or dark, whichever came first. They would watch the big clock downtown, and when it would be close to 6:00, they would run home. We were all expected to be home and ready for dinner with our parents by 6:30 p.m. We did not have air conditioning at home, and when it was very hot, my eldest brother, Walter, would go the Alamo Theater and spend the day in the air-conditioned building watching the movies over and over. When Mama needed him to do his chores, she would call Mr. Leroy Jackson, the theater manager, and ask him to send Walter home.

Byron was my next-oldest brother, and he covered the neighborhood—everyone knew Byron. He would be in charge of taking care of me many times, and we would visit his friends all over the community. I loved being with Byron because he was always entertaining and exciting. He would take me to visit the blacksmith who had a shop at the corner of Church and Mill Streets. This was great fun because he would let us watch him work on horses and make horseshoes.

Mrs. Johnny Redmond, a great lady, was our next-door neighbor. She and my grandmother, Marie Burbridge, grew up in Georgia together. Whenever I visited Mrs. Redmond's home, it always smelled like good food. She made the best pound cakes and fried chicken in the world. As a child, I would be in my yard playing, and I would smell the freshly baked cake. This meant it was time to visit Mrs. Redmond. I can also remember spending the night in her wonderful home, which made you want to explore. She had a slide viewer on which she would allow the neighborhood children to watch

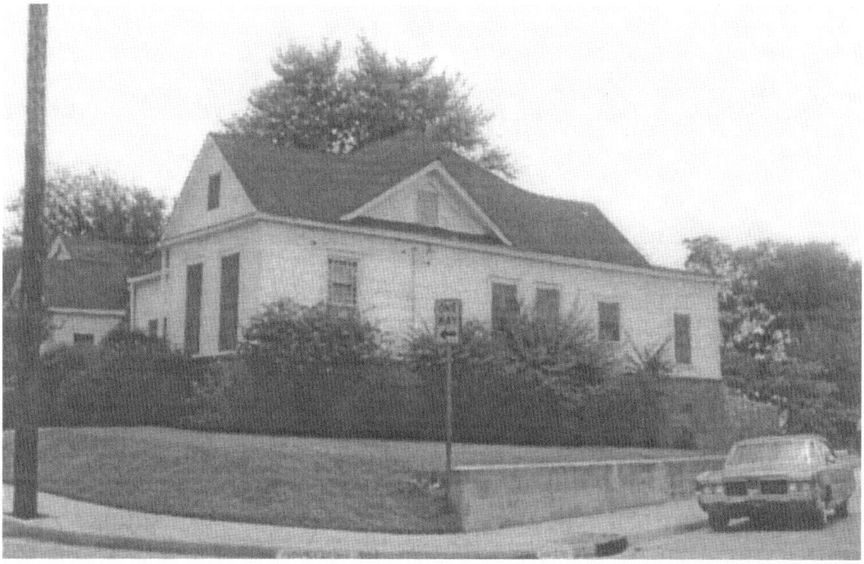

The home of Mrs. Johnny Redmond.

pictures of Paris and other cities in Europe under her close supervision. I would also go over to visit her when she would be working in her yard. Her yard had the most beautiful flowers. On several occasions, I would be the witness to the killing of a chicken. Mrs. Redmond would wring its neck and put a bucket over it until it died. I would sit on her back steps and watch the whole process from beginning to end, including the frying of the chicken.

Another adventure was visiting Mr. Edward Lee's hotel on Church Street near Mill Street, because they had the only television on the street. We children would go to watch the Saturday morning cartoons. Mrs. Addie Lee, Mr. Lee's wife, would be our host, and she would always make us feel welcome.

Chapter 19
Randall Pinkston

From the September 1, 2011 *Jackson Advocate* newspaper:

I was born in Yazoo County but grew up in Jackson in the Farish Street neighborhood, first on Hamilton Street and later on Church Street. I spent a few years and many summers in Yazoo County and Yazoo City with my mother, great-grandmother and sisters. But my childhood was mostly shaped in Jackson, where I was raised by my "other mom and dad," my great-aunt and uncle, Lucy and Warren Wallace.

I attended Central United Methodist Church and Mount Helm Baptist Church. I am an alumnus of Smith Robertson Elementary: (Mr. LaVergne Randolph Sr., principal), Rowan Junior High (Mr. A.N. Jackson, principal) and Lanier High School (Mr. Luther Buckley, principal).

Mr. Randolph once told me that he and his colleagues and their excellent staff never had sufficient resources, but they more than made up for a lack of new textbooks or lab equipment with a passionate commitment to their students. They knew a new day was coming, and they worked hard to make sure that we were ready to take advantage of opportunities which unfolded with the Civil Rights Movement and related federal legislation.

When we moved to Church Street, our neighbors included Mr. Frank Conic, who owned a home on the corner of Church and Dreyfus Streets; Mr. Duke Williams (Walter H. Williams, president, Security Life Insurance Company), who lived on the corner of Church and High; and Dr. R.O. Williams, who lived near Church and Lamar. On the other side of High

Street was a stylish couple who also attended Mount Helm—James and his lovely bride, Mrs. Mattie Rundles. Across the street were Mr. and Mrs. Carsie Hall, and next door, Mr. and Mrs. Sidney Tharp.

One of Jackson Advocate*'s recent columns mentioned one of my favorite people, a wonderful mentor and educator, Mrs. Gustava Mason Gooden. She was my Sunday school teacher, choir director and much more. She and her husband, Mr. James Gooden, took a personal interest in my education and development. Mr. Gooden was the first person I met who had a library in his home. I recall one afternoon when we pulled down one of Halliburton's travelogues. Mr. Gooden told me that by reading Halliburton's books, he had traveled the world without leaving his home. I soon understood that he was impressing on me the importance of using books to transport me to other places to see other possibilities. Mrs. Gooden arranged my first independent long-distance travel as a delegate to the National Sunday School and Baptist Training Union Convention in Tulsa, Oklahoma. I traveled by train via Memphis. I still remember my excitement and some of the people I met during that glorious week in Tulsa.*

I must also mention Miss Ruth Roman and her staff at the Carver Branch Library at the corner of Church and Mill Streets. It was my favorite place; I loved it even more than the Alamo Theater and the Bethlehem Center wading pool. Finally, I should also mention a distinguished gentleman with white hair who visited my mom and dad. He would compliment me and always tell me to "ask questions, young man, ask questions." The distinguished gentleman was attorney Sidney Redmond Jr., who owned our home and other real estate holdings throughout Jackson.

I loved my childhood in the Farish Street neighborhood. Whenever I come home, I drive around the old neighborhood, sad that the homes are mostly abandoned and the stores and businesses are shuttered. Still, I keep in my heart warm memories of the wonderful people who made up the village that nourished me and so many others.

Chapter 20

Elijah Slaughter

As a child growing up, I remember Church Street as being a community full of life, plenty of professional people and many lovely, stately homes. Prominent citizens lived on the street, like the Redmonds, Duke Williams, Doris and Carsie Hall, Sidney Tharp, the Rundles, the Conics, Elma Slaughter and the Shinaults.

On the side of Church Street, next to the cemetery, was Mount Helm, the oldest black church in Jackson, pastored by Reverend A.L. Rice. On the other end of Church Street, next to Mill Street, were Dr. A.B. Britton and Frances Britton and their lovely children. Mrs. Rundles, the mother of James Rundles, was their babysitter for many years.

The professionals living on Church Street included doctors, lawyers, teachers, barbers, restaurant owners and other successful businessmen. Church Street was a prodigious name to have on a resume in the glory days.

My family owned the house at 134 East Church Street. I believe it was built by my uncle, Jim Slaughter, a local contractor. He also built a replica of 134 East Church Street at 193 Whitfield Street.

Uncle Jim was married to Anna Farish of the Farish family for whom Farish Street is so named. As the Great Depression deepened and times got really hard, Uncle Jim either sold or transferred this house to his brother Ernest H. Slaughter, my daddy. Ernest Slaughter was a postal worker with seven children, and all of this notable family attended Mount Helm Baptist Church for many decades. Mr. Slaughter was the head deacon, and his wife, Carrie M. Davis Slaughter, was a deaconess. If nobody showed up on rainy nights or on occasional snow days, Reverend Rice always noted the Slaughters in attendance—even though we lived in Tougaloo, Mississippi, and we really didn't have good transportation (everybody remembered our rusty pick-up truck with the top missing).

Elma Slaughter resided at 134 East Church Street for many years. She was a teacher at Smith Robertson School and taught the third grade. It was very convenient for her to walk the short distance from 134 Church Street to the school. This continued for many years until she finally relocated to 1106 Wiggins Street in west Jackson. In the late 1950s, the professionals began to relocate, and some died. Slowly, the street that was once grand began to erode. The stately homes were rented in many instances. This happened to 134 Church Street. Ernest Slaughter converted the house into a duplex, and several families rented it over the years. Later, Dorothy Slaughter Young, Ernest Slaughter's eldest daughter, became the owner and continued to rent the house. It was not a profitable experience, and at one time she was forced to face a shotgun pointed at her by one of her renters. This did it for Dorothy. She gave up being a landlord. The house began to fall into bad times. A very large tree fell on the roof and caused lots of damage.

Marie Slaughter Fouche, Ernest Slaughter's daughter from California, relocated after retirement to 134 Church Street. She transformed the house to its old glory. After spending money and time, she realized the street was deteriorating and that others did not repair their run-down homes. She was also having problems with theft. To the best of my knowledge, Marie was the last Slaughter to occupy the house around 1985–95. The house was then sold to one of the neighbors.

I have fond memories of Church Street. I remember Principal John Shinault at the deaf school. Mrs. Shinault was a teacher and musician. Also attending and belonging to Mount Helm was James Gooden. Mr. Gooden was a scholar and later took a high position with Jackson Public Schools. He became the second superintendent of the Negro schools. He replaced O.B. Cobbins, who was forced to leave the city for allegedly selling jobs and because of his hesitation in the firing of Gladys Noel Bates. Mrs. Gooden was a noted musician and teacher.

I believe that Freddie Waits also lived on Church Street. He was a noted jazz drummer with a nationally known band. Freddy died many years ago. [Freddie Douglas Waits, a hard bop and post-bop drummer, was born on April 27, 1943, in Jackson, Mississippi, and died on November 18, 1989, in New York City.]

Chapter 21

Charlotte Shinault-Coleman

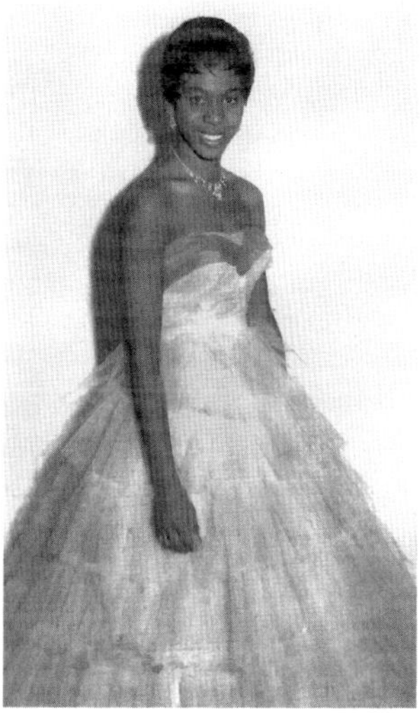

Johnetta Shinault, the first African American model for the Coca Cola Bottling Company.

I was born August 24, 1947. I lived at 244 East Church Street. Our house was located between those of Mr. and Mrs. Bell and Mrs. Evangeline Williams. Church Street was a long street, stretching from Lamar/Grayson to Mill Street, with a library and hotel at one end and a church, Mount Helm Baptist Church, at the other. There were many colorful people living here.

I have many fond memories of those days: trick-or-treating on Halloween, sporting the fashions of the era at Easter, dinner on the grounds at Mount Helm with Reverend Rice, receiving my pierced ears from Dr. Britton, Girl Scout meetings with Mrs. Doris Hall and purchasing cosmetics from Mr. Conic's Beauty Supply store. At the corner of Farish and Church Streets was the Grocery Store (Bob Salvage), popular for all the varieties of foodstuffs needed by our families.

The family home of our local insurance agent/businessman, Duke Williams, was located at the corner of High Street and Church Street. Church Street was a melting pot of people. It included educators, lawyers, doctors, businessmen and entertainment gurus. Everyone looked out for and after each other. It was a community of love, respect and dignity. Our disciplines on life were formed here. We were encouraged to be free thinkers and to expand our horizons. Our dreams were formed and designed here. I didn't realize how important Church Street was to me then—I am thankful for my origins there.

Unit 4

Wives' Tales

In order to do a little bragging, a little hero worshiping or to criticize, the African Americans of Church Street, during the early days, utilized a sophisticated pipeline known as wives' tales. An old wives' tale is a type of urban legend similar to a proverb that is generally passed down by old wives to a younger generation. Such tales usually consist of superstition, folklore or unverified claims with exaggerated and/or untrue details. The origins of the rumors were seldom traceable or were told in a manner that would cause problems for African Americans in the Jim Crow South.

In the early days of Church Street, wives' tales covered a wide range of rumors about family members relating to lawsuits, family tragedies, scandals, escorts to the city limits, shameful acts, going the extra mile and the "Blue Vein Society."

Chapter 22
Lawsuits

There were no shortages of lawsuits filed against high-profile family members of the early days of Church Street. One particular case that caught the fancy of many African Americans involved the wife of a well-known African American lawyer and a prominent African American dentist.

Annie L. Mhoon vs. Dr. A.H. McCoy

Mrs. Mhoon filed a libel lawsuit against Dr. A.H. McCoy on January 11, 1941. The case was immediately dismissed in a summary judgment decision. However, Mrs. Mhoon was able to get the judge to reinstate the lawsuit on September 17, 1941. Nearly one year later, the case ended with a favorable decision for Dr. McCoy. But litigation did not end here, as Mrs. Mhoon appealed the case to a higher court. Unfortunately, records of the third trial were not available (after all, the third trial was filed over seventy years ago).

The wives' tale version of the libel suit contends that while many considered Dr. McCoy, a single, successful dentist, a good catch for some single young lady, Mrs. Annie L. Mhoon allegedly, in a meeting with several women, stated in so many words that Dr. McCoy was not the ideal catch because he was already married to a lady with one child who lived in another state. Evidently, Dr. McCoy was made aware of her statement. He immediately agreed to an interview with editor Percy Greene of the *Jackson Advocate*. The interview appeared on the front page of the newspaper and read in pertinent part, "The case which grew out of a published denial by Dr. McCoy of rumors to the effect that 'the reason he would not marry her was because he was already married, and had a living wife and child' was the first case of its kind in the history of the state."

Some of the most prominent African Americans in the medical field testified at these trials, and the case lasted three years.

Posey vs. Mhoon

In the early 1940s, Mr. Posey, an African American postal worker, filed a lawsuit against his lawyer, W.L. Mhoon, who was also an African American. In accordance with rumors floated by wives' tales, Mr. Posey paid attorney Mhoon $650 for an effort toward getting him promoted to postmaster. When Mr. Posey was denied the promotion, he filed the lawsuit to retrieve his $650. The rumor during this period was that a job or promotion could be purchased if the right contact were made.

O.B. Cobbins vs. Bishop Major Conic

In 1943, everyone was getting ready for the National Convention of the Church of Christ (Holiness) U.S.A. It was at this convention that the senior bishop was selected. Supporters of Bishop O.B. Cobbins selected Jackson, Mississippi, as the site of the national convention, as Jackson was normally the host city. However, at the same time, supporters of Bishop Major Conic selected the city of Chicago for the site. Chicago eventually prevailed as the site, and O.B. Cobbins filed for an injunction in court. He lost, and Bishop Major Conic was named the senior bishop of the Church of Christ (Holiness) U.S.A.

The State of Mississippi vs. Eddie James

In 1948, eighteen-year-old Eddie James murdered Mr. J.E. Conic Sr., the owner of City Barber Shop on North Farish Street and patriarch of the

Conic family of Church Street, and stole his car. Eddie James was tried in 1949 and convicted of murder. He was sentenced to twenty-five years in the Mississippi State Penitentiary. The young lady who rode to Chicago with Eddie James in the stolen car was not charged with anything. After serving twenty-three years of a twenty-five-year sentence, Eddie James was released from prison in 1972. He was forty-two years old.

The wives' tale maintains that a well-known juke joint owner had a girlfriend being released from the state penitentiary in 1972. The girlfriend asked her former boss and boyfriend to meet her at the Trailway Bus Station on this particular day at 3:00 p.m. She also told the boyfriend that Eddie James was being released and would be on the same bus. Rumors indicate that the juke joint owner visited J.E. Conic Jr. at his barbershop near Church Street and shared the information about Eddie James's 3:00 p.m. arrival. He offered his Colt 44 to Conic Jr. and told him to meet the bus at 3:00 p.m. and shoot down Eddie James as he got off the bus. Conic Jr. thanked the juke joint owner for his interest and told him "straight up" that Mr. James had served his time and that his father's death was a closed issue.

Chapter 23

Tragedies

In the early days, those glorious families of Church Street lived decent lives, and some families even lived the "good life" that equaled that of the middle-class whites who lived on North State and West Capitol Streets. But even the good life did not spare those glorious families of Church Street from heartbreaking tragedies.

- As previously reported, Mr. J.E. Conic Sr. was murdered, and it took several days before his body was recovered from a lake located behind a lumberyard in west Jackson.
- The wife of J.E. Conic Jr. died in a housefire on Lynch Street. Rumor has it that a relative in a drunken state accidentally caused the fire.
- A relative of the Conic family of Church Street accidentally shot the son of Reverend Wheaton, the pastor of Central United Methodist Church, whose family also lived on Church Street. Reverend Wheaton's son died from the shooting. Wives' tales of the era set the stage for the shooting as follows: Two boys from the 400 block of Mill Street concocted a "zip gun," a homemade gun that fires real bullets. (A cap gun can be disassembled and a barrel added, turning the toy gun into a real one, and a firing pin can then be added to the hammer to concentrate the force onto the primer of the cartridge. If the cap gun has a strong enough hammer spring, the existing trigger mechanism can be used as is; otherwise, rubber bands may be added to increase the power of the hammer.) The two boys from Mill Street then visited Dr. A.H. McCoy's Ritz Theater on the 600

block of North Farish Street. One of the boys pointed the zip gun at the lady in the ticket cage of the Ritz Theater. An alert employee (ticket collector) who had recently been discharged from the U.S. Navy saw the boy with the zip gun and immediately disarmed the youth. The two boys fled the scene, leaving the zip gun behind. The ticket collector placed the gun on a table near his station and more or less forgot about it. Later that same day, Reverend Wheaton's son and the relative of the Conic family visited the Ritz Theater and came across the zip gun. While inspecting the weapon, the Conic relative accidentally disengaged the trigger, which discharged a bullet that fatally struck Reverend Wheaton's son. Although there was no outward friction between the Wheaton and Conic families after the shooting, the Conic relative was sent to New York to live.

Chapter 24

Scandals

Wives' tales spewed out several scandalous rumors concerning several family members of Church Street during the glorious days.

- An up-and-coming photographer was arrested and served time in the state penitentiary for receiving stolen goods and passing a bad check.
- The son of a well-known preacher owned a juke joint, and his girlfriend supposedly operated a brothel.
- A well-known African American businessman and part-time funeral home worker was suspected of performing an abortion in a room at the Edward Lee Hotel.
- A returning decorated marine in a drunken state allegedly married a widow with nine children and immediately joined the U.S. Army the next week.
- The well-respected leaders of the Black and Tan Republican Party were allegedly accused of selling federal jobs.
- A state penitentiary superior was allegedly bribed by a well-known African American female executive whose son was serving time. The alleged bribe involved placing the son on kitchen duty.
- A well-known African American female executive was accused of padding the payroll of her department.
- A well-known African American lawyer allegedly caught his wife in a compromising position with a white businessman. He supposedly spanked his wife, and all lived happily thereafter.

- The Grayson Street home of Mrs. Betty Marino, a well-respected teacher, was converted into a transient hotel.
- Several prominent African American professionals were asked by white authorities, in no uncertain terms, to depart from the state of Mississippi.
- A prominent African American school administrator was asked to leave Mississippi after being accused of allegedly selling jobs in the school system.
- Two well-known attorneys, a father and his son, were faced with the option of going to jail or leaving the state as a result of their alleged unethical law practices.
- A well-known African American official of the Black and Tan Republican Party escaped the possibility of bodily harm by leaving the state for a new home in Washington, D.C.

Chapter 25

The Extra Mile

Although Mount Helm Baptist Church was the flagship of African American churches in Jackson back in the late 1800s, it was not fully supported by the affluent families of Church Street. On two separate occasions, Mount Helm's declining revenue was salvaged by two African American citizens that were not from Church Street. The first instance involves an African American grocery store owner who entered into a promissory note with the church. The amount of the note is unknown, but apparently the businessman waited over thirty years before demanding payment on the note—and pandemonium broke out because very few members of Mount Helm knew about the outstanding promissory note. The second occasion involves an African American funeral director who, during a slow period in revenue collection, pledged $1,000 a month and paid this amount until his death.

Chapter 26

Blue Vein Society

This idea of a Blue Vein Society originated around 1865, and its inception was based on the mulatto society of that time. Its members were often well-connected freeborn or freed individuals of mixed African, European and, occasionally, Native American blood. To be eligible for membership, one's skin color had to be pale enough that the "blue veins" on the underside of the arm were visible.

During the glory days of Church Street, several professional African Americans attempted to organize a Blue Vein Society. The theory was first discussed in an affluent African American church. After the discussion, the governor of the state was contacted, and the idea died in his office. Although there was no legal action taken on the Blue Vein proposal, the 500 block of Pascagoula Street developed a community of "high yellow" neighbors.

Unit 5

Decline

Chapter 27

The Fall of Church Street

The slow decline of Church Street occurred over approximately fifteen years, culminating in the late 1960s. Long gone is the crimeless community of elegant homes and prestigious families.

In the early days, West Church Street was a bustling community of twenty homes and businesses. West Church Street extended from Mill Street to North Farish Street. Even Conic's Superior Barber Shop, located on the corner of West Church Street and North Farish Street, closed its doors many years ago, and recently the building was demolished. Only historic Farish Street Baptist Church, located on the corner of West Church and Farish Streets, is still standing.

East Church Street suffered the same fate of deteriorating buildings. East Church Street was a community of approximately fifty homes that extended from North Farish Street to Lamar Street.

In the early days, a white-owned business built forty shotgun-style houses in the Farish Street district: ten on North Farish Street, ten on Bloom Court, ten on Bloom Street and ten on East Church Street between North Farish and Bloom Street. The City of Jackson renovated these shotgun houses twelve years ago at a cost of $8 million via a federal grant. Unfortunately, many of the houses mysteriously caught fire, and the remaining houses are totally unlivable. Yet this blighted area still stands because the shotgun houses are listed on the National Register of Historical Places.

There are many factors to be considered in explaining the fall of Church Street. Naturally, death among the original families is one of the factors.

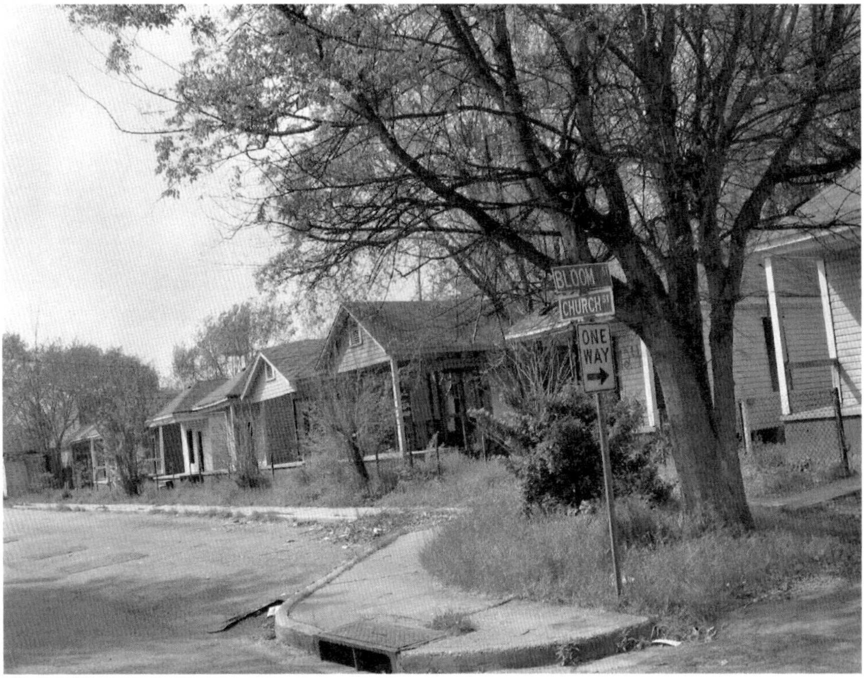

Shotgun-style homes on historic Farish Street.

The Redmonds, Conics, Byrds, Hodges, Topps, Tharps, Perkinses, Brittons, Sally Reynolds, Reverend Rice and Reverend Holland were all influential residents of Church Street during the early days, and after they passed away, many of the children of these influential families moved away to other communities or even other states. Some of them relocated to the states where they attended college or those states that afforded greater job opportunities. For example, Dr. Sidney D. Redmond's son relocated to St. Louis, one of Duke Williams's sons relocated to Houston and one of Edward Lee's sons relocated to Alabama.

Then there were those families who moved away from Church Street into newly developing areas such as Virden Addition, Georgetown, Bel Air and other communities. For instance, Reverend Wendell Taylor moved the Central United Methodist Church parsonage from the 100 block of East Church to the Georgetown community, thus making the old house on Church Street rental property. Dr. A.B. Britton Jr. moved from West Church to Whitfield Mill Road in the Georgetown community, where the new Lanier High School was built. His former home on West Church

Street became rental property. Doris Hall of East Church Street moved to the Bel Air subdivision, and her home also became rental property. Frank Conic of East Church Street moved to Livingston Road near the Virden Addition community. Attorney Sidney Tharp moved to Maple Street in the Georgetown community, and his former home became rental property. Mrs. Nellie Williams, wife of businessman Duke Williams, moved to north Jackson, and her former home became rental property. Eventually, this influx of rental properties gave rise to tenants who did not keep up the property and brought some bad influences into the community.

Amazingly, the establishments that gave rise to Church Street are still standing in modern facilities. The recently renovated Mount Helm Baptist Church is still standing, as is the Farish Street Baptist Church, which was also renovated several years ago. Each church has been in the area over one hundred years.

There are some intrinsic factors to consider in explaining the fall of Church Street. First, there was World War II. Mississippi, like most of America, responded with unbridled patriotism when the Japanese attacked Pearl Harbor in 1941. Thousands of Mississippians entered the armed forces. The City of Jackson alone lost six thousand African Americans to the draft in 1941. During the span of World War II (1941–45), some significant societal changes took place with African Americans in the city of Jackson. For the first time, African American women played a significant role in the state's industrial work force.

The African American male in the armed forces found that his duties were that of a subservient soldier to his white counterpart. However, in 1943, the African American soldiers were allowed to actually engage the enemy (German and Japanese) in armed combat, and the African American Tuskegee Airmen distinguished themselves. Also, the Red Ball Express played a major role in General Patton's success. The Tuskegee Airmen, in their fighter airplanes, did an outstanding job providing protection for the B-47 bombers. The Red Ball Express drove gas trucks on the battlefield, providing fuel for General Patton's tanks.

On June 22, 1944, the Servicemen's Readjustment Act, commonly known as the GI Bill of Rights, became law. By the time the original GI Bill ended in July 1956, 7.8 million World War II veterans had participated in an education or training program, and 2.4 million veterans had home loans backed by the Veterans' Administration (VA). Many of these veterans were, of course, African Americans in Jackson, Mississippi. The GI Bill provided college or vocational education for returning World War II African

American veterans, as well as one year of unemployment compensation. It also provided many different types of loans for returning veterans to buy homes and start businesses. Since the original act, the term has come to include other veteran benefit programs created to assist veterans of both subsequent wars and peacetime service.

In 1948, President Harry S. Truman's Executive Order 9981 ordered the integration of the armed forces, a major advance in civil rights. Using the executive order meant that Truman could bypass Congress. Representatives of the white "Solid South" Democrats would likely have stonewalled related legislation.

All of the above events gave the African American male in Jackson, Mississippi, a new attitude toward segregation. Many of them became skilled workers due to the GI Bill. The subservient role to their white counterpart was on the decline. For the first time, they saw Church Street as being part of the establishment that hindered their progress. In mass numbers, the African Americans began an exit from the inner city.

Then, in 1954, the murder of Emmett Till in north Mississippi added another facet to this new African American attitude—the need to be free. Then there was the preacher from Atlanta, Georgia, who motivated the African Americans toward reaching their goal.

Finally, in 1964, President Johnson, a southerner, pushed the Civil Rights Bill of 1964 through Congress, thus making it the law of the land. The United States Equal Employment Opportunity Commission, created by the historic Civil Rights Act of 1964, succeeded in opening the doors of opportunity for countless African Americans in Jackson, Mississippi.

The Civil Rights Act of 1964 was a landmark piece of legislation in the United States that outlawed major forms of discrimination against blacks and women, including racial segregation. It ended unequal application of voter registration requirements and racial segregation in schools, in the workplace and in facilities that served the general public. Powers given to enforce the act were initially weak but were supplemented during later years. Congress asserted its authority to legislate under several different parts of the U.S. Constitution, principally its power to regulate interstate commerce under Article One (Section 8), its duty to guarantee all citizens equal protection of the laws under the Fourteenth Amendment and its duty to protect voting rights under the Fifteenth Amendment. The act was signed into law by President Lyndon B. Johnson, who would later sign the landmark Voting Rights Act into law.

In summary, the decline and, subsequently, the fall of Church Street is not based upon one reason but a combination of reasons. We would be remiss, however, if we did not mention that it was Church Street during the early days that planted the seed that grew into equal opportunity for African Americans in the city of Jackson. This qualified group of African American citizens could perform all types of jobs within the city—that is, if they had not been denied the opportunity because of race. On the other hand, this same seed planted by the early inhabitants of Church Street led to the demise of the glory days of the street, as with success, many African Americans moved away.

Unit 6

TRAILBLAZERS

This section focuses on present-day successful African Americans of Jackson with direct ties to those amazing families of Church Street.

Chapter 28

Dennis Charles Sweet III

Dennis Sweet's ties with those glorious families of Church Street had its beginning at 234 East Church Street in the home of the Perkins family. This family produced Dennis's mother, Grace Britton Sweet, and his uncle, Dr. A.B. Britton Jr.

Barber Wright, a *Jackson Advocate* staff writer, best described Dennis in the following statement:

> *Getting the job done appears to come easy for top Jackson attorney Dennis Sweet III. And when the question arises "Is he good?" Sweet says, "I let my work speak for me. I chose to do public interest work so that I could give back to the community."*
>
> *Dennis C. Sweet III heads Sweet and Associates Law Firm.*
>
> *With a 95 percent win record in trying personal injury and product liability cases, and punitive damages in the millions, it's no wonder people are talking about "how Sweet it is" when it comes to civil litigator Dennis Sweet. It's no wonder he has grabbed the national spotlight with victories such as a $144 million verdict against Ford Motor Co. (the largest wrongful death verdict in Mississippi's history) and a $400 million verdict against American Home Product, makers of the Fen-Phen diet pill, as well as a $23 million verdict for a couple with a brain-damaged child; a $4.5 million wrongful death malpractice verdict against Hospice Ministries in the death of a woman who, improperly diagnosed with cancer, died from an overdose of painkillers; and a $23 million verdict against the Jackson*

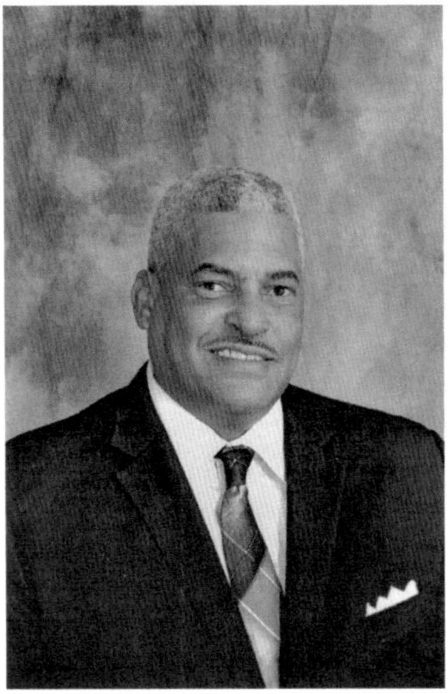

Dennis Charles Sweet III.

Marriott Hotel and the City of Jackson for the shooting of an unarmed man by an off-duty Jackson Police officer.

On December 13, 2011, Dennis Sweet enjoyed another victory: on Tuesday, the Mississippi Court of Appeals affirmed a $4.6 million Hinds County jury verdict in Miss. Baptist Health Systems vs. Kelly. *This was a pre-tort reform cap case. Ellen Kelly died as a result of exposure to latex during a surgery procedure at Baptist Hospital in Jackson. A form from an earlier surgery procedure indicated that Ellen was allergic to latex. The jury rendered a verdict against Baptist but exonerated the doctor defendants.* Black Enterprise *magazine (November 2003) featured a story about Dennis. The magazine named Dennis Sweet III as being the nation's top lawyer.*

Dennis graduated from St. Joseph Catholic High School. He received a degree in economics in 1977 from Tougaloo College and a jurisprudence doctorate degree from the George Washington University School of Law in 1980.

Chapter 29

Randall Pinkston

Randall Pinkston's tie with those glorious families of Church Street had its beginning on East Church Street in a house owned by attorney Sidney Redmond Jr. Pinkston's great-aunt and -uncle, Lucy and Warren Wallace, lived in this house and raised Randall. At a very young age, Randall had a *Jackson Daily News* paper route. This paper route gave Randall the opportunity to get acquainted with many of the people in his neighborhood. After completing college and gaining recognition as a prominent newsperson, Randall would always return to Jackson for speaking engagements. In each speech, he would reflect on his life and the people on Church Street: "Church Street was indeed a village in every sense of the word. I was blessed to grow up with the support and guidance of Mr. Lewis Perkins and his wonderful neighbors."

Randall Pinkston joined CBS News in 1990. Since 1994, he has been a New York–based CBS News correspondent. He has been assigned to Newspath since February 2010, providing reports to CBS-owned and -operated stations and affiliates.

Pinkston has covered many major stories of the past decade for CBS News, including coverage of the Chilean earthquake; Tiger Woods's return to the Augusta National Golf Club and the Masters Tournament; the first anniversary of the Haiti earthquake; the final launch of NASA's shuttle *Discovery* from the Kennedy Space Center; and the postwar reconstruction of Iraq. He has also reported on the war in Afghanistan from the front lines in Tora Bora and Jalalabad; the devastating earthquake in Turkey;

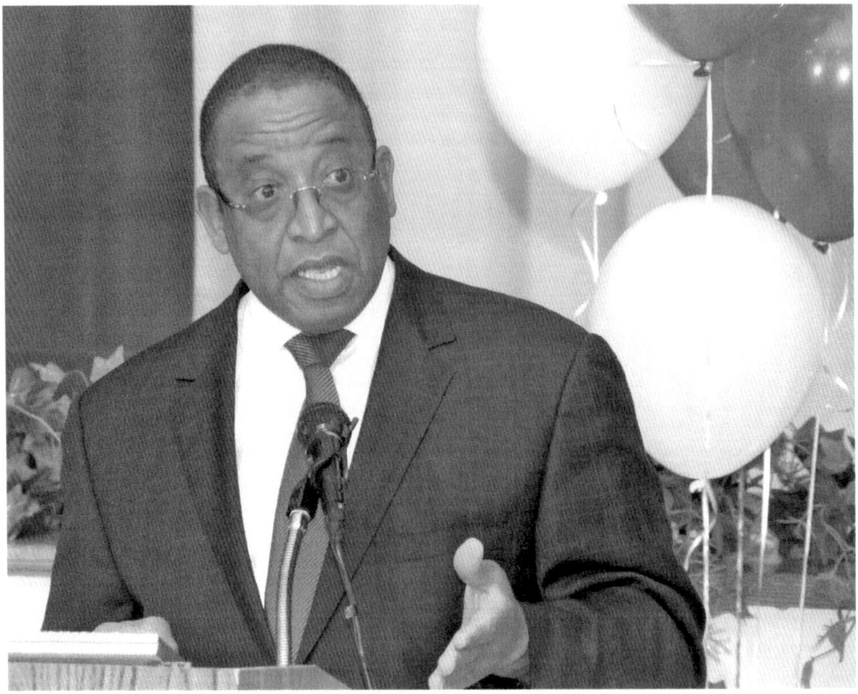

Randall Pinkston speaking at the ninetieth birthday party of Mr. L.B. Buckley (former principal of Lanier High School). *Courtesy of Jay Johnson.*

the Albanian refugee crisis in Kosovo and the U.S. military participation in the Balkans; Saddam Hussein's refusal to allow U.N. inspection officers to enter Iraq; the U.S. intervention in Haiti; the Susan Smith trial, during which he broke the story of her arrest and landed the first interview with her ex-husband, David Smith; the Freemen siege in Montana; and the Unabomber story.

Pinkston is the recipient of three national Emmy Awards and two for local news coverage. In 1996, he received an Emmy for Outstanding Investigative Journalism and the Edward R. Murrow Award from the RTNDA for the documentary *CBS Reports: Legacy of Shame*, in which he served as the reporter. The broadcast was inspired by the landmark 1960 CBS documentary *Harvest of Shame*, with Edward R. Murrow. Pinkston also won Emmy Awards for coverage of the death of Princess Diana in 1998 and for his coverage of the TWA Flight 800 disaster in 1997.

Prior to his New York assignment, Pinkston was based in the CBS News Washington, D.C. bureau (1990–94), where he joined the network as a White

House correspondent. The move to Washington came just one month before the start of the Persian Gulf War, and almost immediately, Pinkston became a fixture on *CBS This Morning* and CBS Radio while reporting on the war. He spent two years at the White House covering President George H.W. Bush, including many presidential trips abroad. Pinkston broke the story of Bush's illness while dining with Japanese prime minister Kiichi Miyazawa.

Chapter 30

Denise Sweet Owens

Denise Sweet Owens is the sister of attorney Dennis Sweet III. Likewise, Denise's ties with those glorious families of Church Street had its beginning at 234 East Church Street at the home of the Perkins family. This family produced Denise's mother, Grace Britton Sweet, and her uncle, Dr. A.B. Britton Jr.

Judge Denise Sweet Owens graduated from St. Joseph Catholic High School. She then entered Christian Brothers College for one year and completed her college education in 1976 at Tougaloo College, where she obtained her BA degree. She received a doctor of jurisprudence from the George Washington School of Law in 1979.

Denise became a partner in the firm of Owens and Byrd. In 1989, with her community's support, she was elected Chancery Court judge. She is currently a sitting Chancery Court judge in Hinds County. She was one of the first females to hold the position in the state of Mississippi.

The Chancery Court has always been the separate court of equity (as distinguished from the circuit law court) in Mississippi, and the chancellor generally hears cases without a jury. Judge Owens is often asked to hear cases in other parts of the state. Although the requirements of a Chancery Court judge are broad and complicated, Judge Owens has served as chancellor since 1989.

Judge Owens is past secretary, vice-chair and chairperson of the Mississippi Conference of Chancery Judges. She is a member of the Mississippi Bar, the Mississippi Bar Foundation, the National Association of

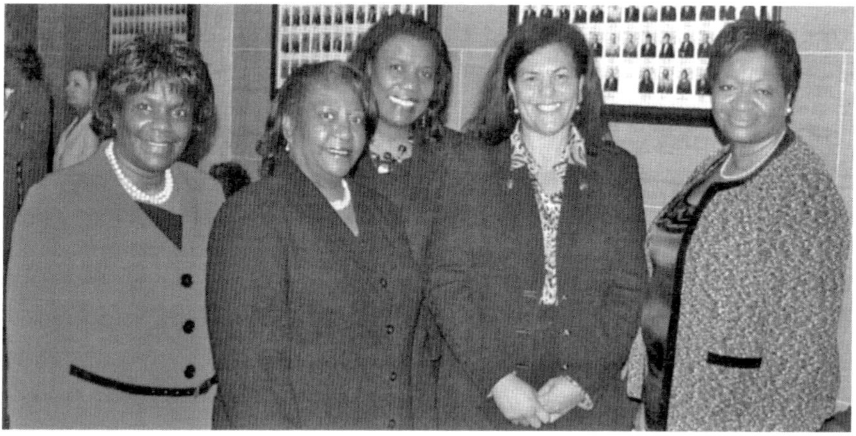

From left to right: Judges Ermea Russell, Lillie Blackmon Sanders, Betty W. Sanders, Denise Owens and Patricia Wise being honored as the first African American women to serve on the Court of Appeals, Circuit and Chancery Branches.

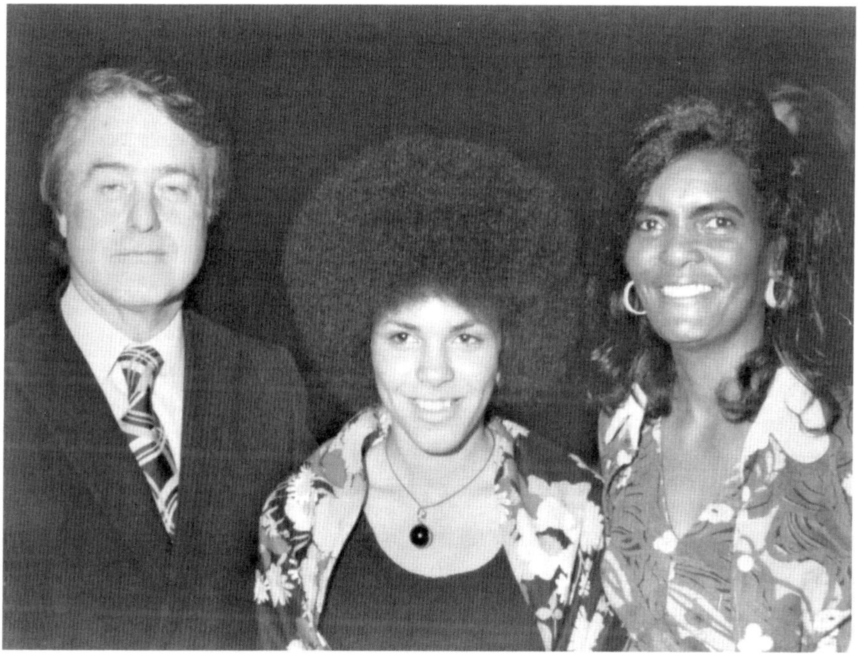

Sergeant Shiver, Denise Owens and Grace Sweet. Denise received an award for being the most outstanding Catholic teenager in the South Western Conference for the Catholic Youth Organization.

Women Judges and the Magnolia Bar. She was appointed as co-chairperson of the Mississippi Access to Justice Commission. She is also a member of the American Bar and the National Bar. She was the recipient of the 2010 Chief Justice Award from the Mississippi Supreme Court, the 2009 Mississippi Volunteer Lawyers Pioneer Award, the 2010 Tougaloo College Meritorious Leadership Award, the 2006 Hinds County Bar Judicial Innovation Award, the 2003 Mississippi Bar Fellow and the 2002 Magnolia Bar Government Service Award.

Chapter 31

Albert B. Britton III

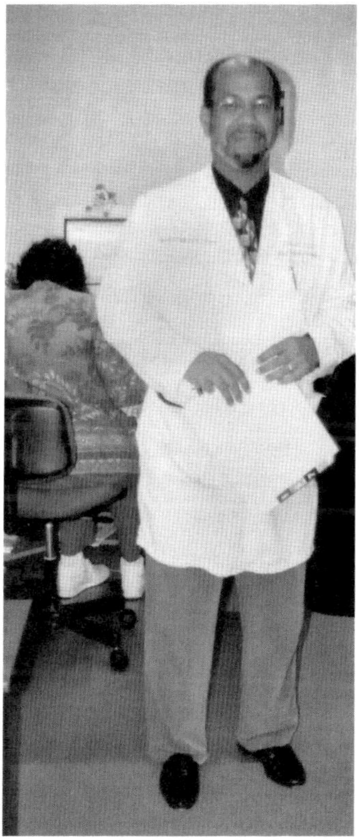

Albert B. Britton III, MD.

The legacy of the Britton family had its beginning at 234 East Church Street in the home of the Perkins family. Dr. A.B. Britton Jr., the father of our trailblazer, Dr. Albert B. Britton III, started his family and legacy on West Church Street.

Dr. Albert B. Britton III was born on July 28, 1949, to Dr. A.B. Britton Jr. and Frances W. Britton of West Church Street in Jackson, Mississippi. Dr. Britton III's connection to the glory days of Church Street is that he is the son of the legendary Dr. Britton.

Dr. Britton III graduated from St. Francis Preparatory High School in Spring Grove, Pennsylvania, in 1967. He received a BS degree with a minor in chemistry from Howard University in 1971. In 1976, he received a degree of medicine from the University of Cincinnati Medical School. In 1979, Dr. Britton III completed his postgraduate medical training at the University of Mississippi Medical Center in Jackson, Mississippi. Most of Dr. Albert

B. Britton III's training in internal medicine occurred at the GV Sonny Montgomery Medical Center in Jackson.

Since 2007, Dr. Britton III has been the medical director and practicing physician in internal medicine for Sterling Medical Corporation of Wilmington, North Carolina. Like his father, he exhibits that Britton fighting spirit. He has a lifetime membership with the NAACP. He served as chairman of the legislative council for the Mississippi Medical and Surgical Association for four years and also served as the state medical director of American Medical Plans of Mississippi, Inc. He was also a member of the Executive Committee at the Mississippi Baptist Medical Center (1997–98).

Additionally, Dr. Britton III has been very active in community service. He was a founding member and first president of the Farish Street Revitalization Association and the Farish Street Development Corporation. In 2000, he was a member of the Parents Alliance for Challenged Children.

Dr. Britton III is licensed to practice medicine in two states, Mississippi and North Carolina, with current DEA number, ACLS Certification and ATLS Certification.

Chapter 32

Selika M. Sweet

Dr. Selika M. Sweet is the sister of attorney Dennis Sweet III and Chancery Court judge Denise Sweet Owens, the first cousin of Dr. Albert B. Britton III and the niece of Dr. Albert B. Britton Jr. Dr. Selika's ties with those glorious families of Church Street originated at 234 East Church Street in the home of the Perkins family. The Perkins family produced Selika's mother, Grace Britton Sweet, and her uncle, Dr. A.B. Britton Jr.

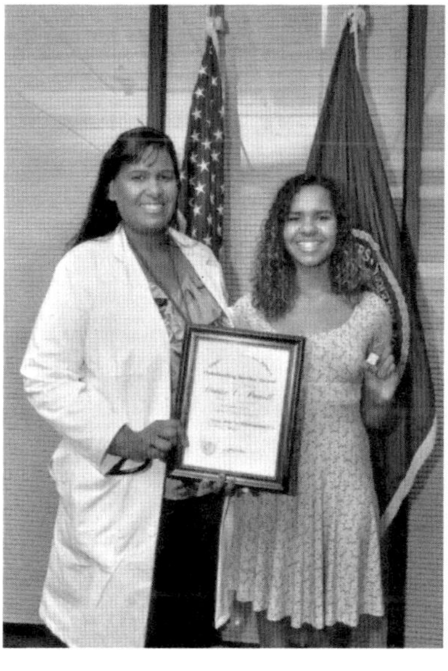

Selika M. Sweet and her daughter, Denise E. Powell. Denise received an award for outstanding service from the Department of Veteran Affairs.

Dr. Sweet is currently employed at the Veteran Administration Medical Center in Biloxi, Mississippi, where she is the director of the Women's Clinic. Dr. Sweet has over twenty years' experience in family medicine.

Dr. Sweet attended St. Joseph Catholic High School and graduated from William B. Murray High School in Jackson in 1979. She attended Dillard University, majored in pre-med and graduated in 1983. Dr. Sweet received her medical degree from Meharry Medical College.

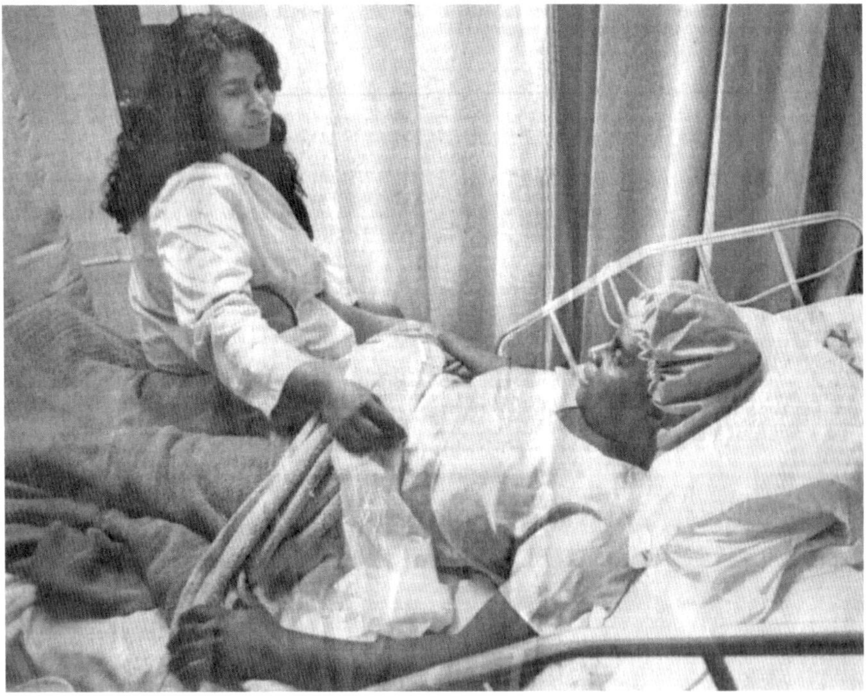

Dr. Selika M. Sweet with a patient.

Dr. Selika M. Sweet completed a three-year residency in family medicine on March 27, 1993, at the Earl K. Long Medical Center in Baton Rouge, Louisiana. It was at this hospital where she distinguished herself as a dedicated physician.

In an interview with the *State Times/Morning Advocate* newspaper, Dr. John Howe, the director of the family practice residency program at Earl K. Long, praised Dr. Sweet for her unselfish decisions in selecting the family practice over a more lucrative practice and choosing to work at Earl K. Long, a charity hospital that is old and dilapidated.

Dr. Sweet is the proud parent of two lovely children, Roe Powell and Denise Powell, who are definitely following the Sweet tradition.

Chapter 33

James Rundles

James Rundles's ties with the glory days of Church Street are direct: he was one of those glorious citizens. He and his wife, Mattie, lived on Church Street, while his mother, Beatrice King Rundles, lived on West Church. Mr. Rundles knew all the newsmakers of Church Street during the early days. For instance, he worked for Percy Greene, the editor and publisher of the *Jackson Advocate* newspaper. He and Dr. Albert B. Britton Jr. were good friends, and he and attorney Carsie Hall belonged to the same social club.

Currently, James Rundles is author of the "Up and Down Farish Street" column for the *Jackson Advocate*, having coauthored and authored this column for nearly sixty-seven years. During those years, James has written about African American news, including achievements in Jackson, Mississippi. Many of his articles have focused on the lives of those glorious families that lived on Church Street in the early days.

At the beginning of World War II, James Rundles was the first African American to join the United States Marines. He was assigned to the legendary Montford Point Marines of Camp Lejeune.

After the war ended in 1945, James became affiliated with Percy Greene and his *Jackson Advocate* newspaper. In 1948, James was elected to head the Community Chest Drive.

In the early 1950s, James became the first news editor for the WOKJ radio station. In the late 1950s, he became the Negro editor for the *Jackson Daily News*. However, all this time, he never relinquished his affiliation with the *Jackson Advocate*.

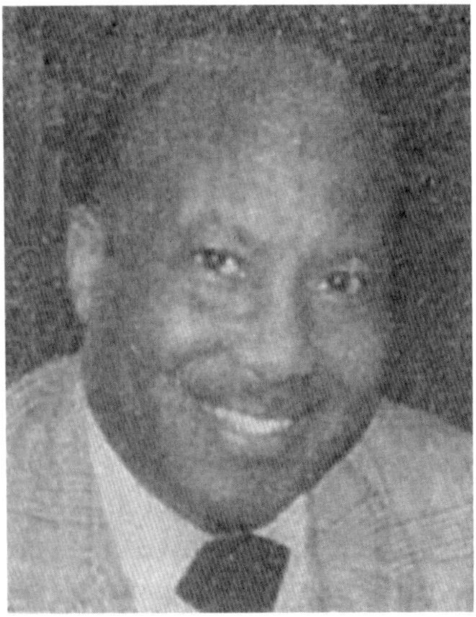

James Rundles.

After Percy Greene died in 1977, his wife, Frances Reed Greene, began running the *Jackson Advocate*, and James continued to write the "Up and Down Farish Street" column. In July 1978, the paper was sold to Mr. Charles Tisdale for $17,000, and James was retained. Charles Tisdale died on July 7, 1997, at age eighty. His wife, Alice Tisdale, then became the publisher, and still James Rundles continued to compose the "Up and Down Farish Street" column.

In 2012, the U.S. Congress awarded the Congressional Gold Medal to James Rundles and the rest of the Montford Point Marines. The Congressional Gold Medal was first granted to General George Washington in 1776, and it has also been awarded to Mother Teresa, the Wright brothers and Thomas Edison. Recently, James Rundles received the Silver Star Medal for his service with the Montford Point Marines.

Appendix I

The Professionals of Church Street, 1940–1950

Resident	Profession
Sally Reynolds	Educator/Teacher
Evangeline Byrd	Midwife
Dr. Sidney Dellon Redmond	Physician/Attorney
Sidney Revels Redmond	Attorney
Dr. A.B. Britton Jr.	Physician
Dr. R.O. Williams	Physician
Percy Abrams	Insurance Executive
John Shinault	Principal/Educator
Walter "Duke" Williams	Insurance Company Owner
Georgia Hodge	Real Estate, Crystal Palace
Jack E. Conic	Barber Shop Owner/Independent Contractor for the *Chicago Defender* and *Pittsburg Courier*
Frank Conic	Owner, Beauty Supply
Carsie Hall	Attorney
Sidney R. Tharp	Attorney

RESIDENT	PROFESSION
Elbert Topp Sr.	Minister, Farish Street Baptist Church
Elbert Topp Jr.	Owner, Tip Top Nite Club
Thelma Topp	Administrator
Doris Tharp Hall	Educator/Administrator
Elma Slaughter	Educator/Teacher
Reverend A.L. Rice	Pastor, Mount Helm Baptist Church/ Professor
Reverend Amos L. Holland	Pastor, Central United Methodist Church
Reverend J.D. Wheaton	Pastor, Central United Methodist Church
Edward Lee Sr.	Owner, Edward Lee Hotel
Albert Butane	Plasterer/Realtor
Lewis Perkins	Plumber
Mr. Mason	Blacksmith
Mrs. Moore	Owner, Moore's Beauty Parlor and School
John Garrnett	Photographer
Mr. Howard	Owner, Bubba Grocery
Mr. Johnson	Locksmith
Catherine Tharp	Educator/Teacher
Nellie Williams	Owner, Penguin Café

Appendix II

Chruch Street's College Students

Student	College
Doris Tharp	Tougaloo College
Carsie Hall	Jackson College
Grace Deloris Britton	Tougaloo College
Sidney R. Tharp	Bluefield State College
Albert Bazaar Britton Jr.	Tougaloo College
Mary Jackson	Jackson College
Ruth Jackson	Jackson College
Edward N. Lee, Jr.	Blue Field State College (West Virginia)
Ruby Thames	Jackson College
Dorothy Lee Lewis	Alcorn College
Grace Weakly	Southern University (Baton Rouge, LA)
Ty Sims	West Virginia State
Annie Kay Lee	Southern University (Baton Rouge, LA)
Ruth Williams	Fisk University
Billy Buckley	Tuskegee Institute
Byron Williams	Tennessee State

STUDENT	COLLEGE
Walker "Duke" Williams Jr.	Talladega College
James Wheaton	Wiley College
Paul Wheaton	Wiley College
Robert Wheaton	Wiley College
Eddie Lee	Tuskegee Institute
Marshall Wheaton	Wiley College
Ruth Solomon	Southern University
Annie Rose Wheaton	Clark College
Ruth Redmond	Howard University
Willie Pinkston	Millsaps College
Catherine Tharp	Jackson College
L'Dina Robinson	Jackson College
Elma Lee	Tougaloo College
Henry Lee	Industrial College (Chicago)
Johnetta Shinault	Tougaloo College
Charlotte Shinault	Arkansas A&M

Bibliography

Cobbins, Otho B., ed. *History of Church of Christ (Holiness) U.S.A., 1895–1965*. New York: Vantage Press, 1966.

Flucker, Turry, and Phoenix Savage. *Images of America: African Americans of Jackson*. Charleston, SC: Arcadia Publishing, 2008.

Middleton, M.P. *The Central Connection: A History of the First One Hundred Years at Central United Methodist Church.* Jackson, MS: Town Square Books, Inc., 1998.

Morias, Herbert. *The History of the Negro in Medicine*. Publisher's Co., 1967.

Pacini, Marina. *Photographs from the Memphis World, 1949–1964*. Jackson: University Press of Mississippi, 2008.

Wilson, Charles H. *God! Make Me A Man*. Boston: The Meador Press, 1950.

Index

C

G

H

J

R

S

About the Authors

Grace Britton Sweet feels that history is vitally important to preserving one's family background. The youngest child of Reverend A.B. and Mrs. Mary (Perkins) Britton Sr., she was reared by her uncle and aunts at 234 East Church Street. She attended Lutheran School on Blair Street and Smith Robertson Junior High School on Bloom Street and in 1948 graduated from Lanier High School. She received her BS from Tougaloo College and MS from Southern University.

Grace is a lifelong resident of Jackson, Mississippi, who spent all of her childhood on Church Street. As an educator, Grace taught in the Jackson public school system, where she worked to instill the love of learning in all her students. The lack of written work on African American families is what prompted her to write this book to help preserve the history of African American families. Her motto is, "You have to know where you came from in order to know where you are going."

Benjamin Bradley Sr. was raised in Jackson, Mississippi, and all of his life has been centered on activities in the historic Farish Street District. He attended the historic Smith Robertson Elementary and Junior High Schools, Tougaloo Preparatory High School and Jackson State University. He served four years in the United States Air Force.

Bradley has witnessed the beginning of World War II, the Korean War, the civil rights movement of the '60s and the election of an African American president—all from a front-row seat in historic Jackson, Mississippi. He became an author by accident. His coauthor suggested many days ago that someone should capture on paper the good life on Church Street back in the day. The coauthor volunteered Bradley to assist her in doing so, and the rest of the story is in this book.